Meditations
of a
Shepherd

Meditations

—— *of a* ——

Shepherd

David T. Demola

VMI PUBLISHERS

Partnering With Christian Authors, Publishing Christian and Inspirational Books

Sister, Oregon

Meditations of a Shepherd © 1990
Revised 2nd Edition Copyright © 2007 by David T. Demola
All rights reserved. Published 2007.

Published by
VMI Publishers
Sisters, Oregon
www.vmipublishers.com

ISBN: 1-933204-50-8
ISBN 13: 978-1-933204-50-5
Library of Congress Control Number: 2007929461
Author contact:
David T. Demola—Author
Faith Fellowship Ministries World Outreach Center, Inc.
2707 Main Street
Sayreville, NJ 08872
732-727-9500

Printed in the USA.

Cover design by Joe Bailen

Dear Believer,

Thank God for His Word! It says in Proverbs 2:3–5 in the Living Bible, "If you want better insight and discernment, and are searching for them as you would for lost money or hidden treasure, then wisdom will be given you, and knowledge of God Himself. You will soon learn the importance of reverence for the Lord and of trusting Him."

What an exciting promise!

Constructed differently than most study aids, this manual is part of my personal study notes. It is a combination of years and years of personal meditation on the power and principles contained in the Old Testament. We have spent literally hundreds of hours studying and editing to put this together in a clear and concise manner.

You will be educated and thoroughly blessed as you go chapter by chapter through the intriguing lives of Old Testament figures, citing their successes and failures and seeing examples of human frailty.

For your benefit, please notice that much of the Scripture is quoted from the Living Bible to enable easy reading and comprehension.

You will never be the same as you are challenged by the Holy Spirit in experiencing the awesomeness of God that is revealed in the Old Testament.

May God richly bless you as you discover the treasure of His precious Word!

Sincerely for Souls,

Pastor David T. Demola

Pastor David T. Demola, Ph.D.

Judges:
A Sad Era in the
History of God's People

RE: Judges 1

In Joshua 24, the book preceding Judges, we find Joshua commanding the people to keep the Word of God and to be faithful to the Lord, just as the Lord told him at the beginning of the book in chapter 1. In chapters 2–12, we see the Israelites entering the Promised Land and uniting to drive out the inhabitants. Then, after the land was divided among twelve tribes, in chapters 13–24, each tribe was responsible for driving out the remaining enemy from its own territory. The book of Judges continues this story, but sadly shows the failure of the people to follow God and do as He commanded.

After the death of Joshua, Israel began to lose its firm grip on the land. Joshua had been more than a military leader; he was a man that trusted God and possessed great spiritual power. Now there was no one to lead the people. Instead of the people putting their trust in the Lord as their leader, they mistrusted Him, and as a result, they could no longer recognize a great leader to succeed Joshua. With God's strength and help, they had conquered many enemies and had overcome every obstacle that was against them. But now, as we will see, the unholy but attractive lifestyle of the Canaanites had become a greater threat to Israel than their military power.

The Canaanites were people who lived in Canaan, and Israel was to drive them out. Some of the tribes had succeeded better than others. Under the leadership of Joshua, they all started out strong but had become sidetracked by fear, weariness, lack of discipline, or the pursuit of their own interests. In fact, later on in Judges 17:6, we will see that everyone began to do what was "right in the sight of their own eyes."

If we are going to overcome with God, we must do better than just make a fast start. Faith is a lifestyle, practiced day by day. We must never lose our focus and become sidetracked, but follow those who, through faith and patience, inherit the promises.

"Drive Them Out"

RE: Judges Chapters 1–3

In Judges 1:21, we see one of many examples in Judges of God's people failing to drive out the enemy. At this point, it was the tribe of Benjamin who failed to drive out the Jebusites. Tribe after tribe failed to drive out the enemy. God had told Abraham, some seven hundred years before, that when Israel would come to Canaan, the gross evil of the people would be ripe for judgment (Genesis 15:16). The Lord knew that if they did not drive these people out of the land, eventually the Canaanites' way of life would affect them. Israel's failure to follow through with God's command would eventually rob them of the promises that God had made to them. Disobedience or rebellion is as the sin of witchcraft, as we shall see in further detail, when we study the life of Saul. In only a short time after Joshua's death, the people were already in fear and lacked the discipline to do what God said. Failure to obey would bring gradual deterioration in their relationship with God. Chapter 1 of Judges explains how the tribes tolerated their enemy and did not execute God's command.

As chapter 2 begins, the angel of the Lord, a special messenger sent directly from Him, speaks to the people. It seems unlikely that he would speak to the several million at one time, particularly since they were scattered. It is more likely that he was speaking to the leaders. His words were stinging and very direct. In effect, God was saying that He made a covenant (or contract) with them at Sinai to make them a special nation,

and to protect them and bless them (Exodus 19:5–8). Their only re-
quirement was to follow Him and obey His laws. But because they had
rejected Him, and had failed to destroy the heathen altars and follow His
directions, they had broken the contract and it was no longer in effect.
God was not saying He did not want them to be His nation, He was saying that He would be different. They could not be the special people He
wanted them to be and He could not fulfill the covenant He made if they
did not obey it. As a result of their disobedience, the Lord told them, "the
heathen will be as a 'thorn in your sides' and you will have testing and
temptation by their hands."

This lesson is a hard one, but one of great importance. Remember
Galatians 6:7, which says, "God is not mocked. Whatsoever a man
soweth, that will he also reap." As regrettable as it may sound, we cannot
escape the consequences if we continue to defy God's rules. Lord God,
help us to walk in the light!

Tears Are Not Enough

RE: Judges 2:4

We found out in our last lesson that the angel of the Lord appeared to the people to give them a message from God concerning the breaking of the covenant. It is interesting to note that there are approximately eighty appearances of angels in the Old Testament, and twenty of them—one quarter of these instances—are found in the book of Judges. Obviously, because there was a strong leader to follow, the people needed divine, supernatural leadership, and this apparently was the way that the Lord chose. Throughout the book of Judges, there is a cycle repeated over and over again: Sin–Servitude–Repentance. The people were constantly running from God, falling into bondage, then running back to God for help. The fruit of Israel's problem could be clearly seen and described with two words:

Compromise: Not doing what God had said (drive out the enemy)

Apostasy: Doing what God said not to do (worship the gods of their enemies)

No wonder the Lord had to constantly speak with them to try to keep them in line. We should also remember that the Lord still loved them even though He had to punish them for their sin; God loves the sinner, but hates his sin.

In Judges 2:4, after the angel gave Israel the message that the covenant was now broken, the people broke into tears and offered sacrifices to the Lord. They knew that they had sinned and they responded with deep sorrow. However, repentance is more than a momentary feeling. Their tears of the moment would mean nothing if, in fact, they were not willing to change their ways and follow God. We know this in part because we can see that they did nothing to train their children (Deuteronomy 6:7–9). Look at the result in Judges 2:10, which says, "So all that generation died, and the next generation did not worship Jehovah as their God." How sad! Not only did they forget God, but they also worshipped heathen gods. They were guilty of compromise and apostasy, and the Bible says that God was angry with them. When we make up our minds to follow God, we must be willing to turn totally around and do all that His Word says to do. Guilt and tears are not enough if we are not willing to turn around and change our ways.

A God of Mercy

RE: Judges 2:15

We hear so much about the grace of God, and rightly so, but most of us have never taken the time to find out about the mercy of God. Remember the contrast of the two definitions:

Grace: Getting from God what we really do not deserve

Mercy: Not getting from God what we really do deserve

For example, Ephesians 2:8, 9 tells us of the saving grace of God, afforded to us for salvation; "By grace (the unmerited favor of God) are ye saved through faith." We also read in Hebrews 2:17 that Jesus is our "merciful high priest to make reconciliation for his people," or, in other words, He forgives us even though we do not deserve to be forgiven.

This is surely the case in Judges 2:15, 16 in the Living Bible translation, which says, "So now when the nation of Israel went out to battle against its enemies, the Lord blocked their path. He had warned them about this, and in fact had vowed that He would do it." Out of mercy, the Lord continued in verse 16, "But when the people were in this terrible plight, the Lord raised up judges to save them from their enemies." Their sin deserved punishment, yet God provided a way of escape by raising up specially anointed judges who would indeed be their rescue, or their "instruments of mercy."

This statement of God "raising up judges" is parenthetical, meaning it describes what the rest of the book is about in short detail, then chapter by chapter—the step-by-step stories of individuals and incidences of this particular period of time in Jewish history. One of the saddest verses found in this context is verse 17. It reads, "Yet (or, in spite of God's effort to raise up judges) even then Israel would not listen to the judges, but broke faith with Jehovah by worshipping other gods. How quickly they turned away from the true faith of their ancestors, for they refused to obey God's commands." Although God did everything He could do to save them, the people stubbornly did what they wanted. Their sin was great, yet God's mercy was abundant to preserve them. The Bible says, "His mercies are new every morning." Thank God for His mercy to us. Without it, none of us would still be around.

Serving God When No One is Looking

RE: Judges 2:15–23

As we learned in the previous lessons, God's mercy was abundant to Israel in the midst of their apostasy and sin. Why did the people turn so quickly from their faith in God? It seems as if from the beginning of the nation, just after coming out of Egypt, the people wanted their gods to be visible, like the heathen nations around them. First, it was the golden calf with Aaron, and it grew progressively worse as the people yearned to be the same as the nations around them. While the Lord wanted them to be a "peculiar" (special, purchased) people, they wanted to be ordinary and mix in with the complacency of the world.

Carefully read chapter 2, verses 18–20. Here we see Israel being rescued by the various judges from their enemies because God heard the groanings of the Israelites under their oppressors, and He was moved with mercy and compassion to help them as long as the judge lived. When the judge would die, the people would turn from what was right and would behave even worse than their ancestors by worshipping heathen gods and returning to the evil customs of the nations around them. The Israelites seemed to serve the Lord when a judge was watching them. Similarly, it is not enough to serve God when someone is watching you. In fact, it is harmful and meaningless, because the motive is wrong. Remaining loyal to God means more than momentary loyalty. It must be permanent. If we are devoted to Him, it means that there must be consistency. We cannot yield to the pressure of things and people around us when the going gets rough. We must determine to remain faithful to our faithful God who never changes.

In verses 20–23, we see that the Lord is angry again, and He says, "I will not drive these heathen enemies (nations) out from the land, but will use them to test the people to see who will trust me." You see, once we make up our minds to do our own thing, we literally forfeit the blessings of God. He was prepared to drive the nations out and was certainly more than able to do so. When we disobey the Word of the Lord, we open ourselves up for the cursings of God (Deuteronomy 27, 28).

Let us be wise, serving God all the time, so that the blessings will come on us and overtake us, and the door to our enemy, the Devil, will be tightly shut.

God's Mercy in Perilous Times

RE: Judges 3

In this third chapter of Judges, there are two incidents of victory for the people of God after they sinned and turned from the Lord. As a matter of fact, the Holy Spirit, the literal writer of Scripture, makes it very clear in verses 1–8 that once again God's people failed to follow His instruction concerning the enemy in this new Promised Land; to drive them out. Again, we see the sinful results.

In verse 6, we read that they intermarried and accepted their spouses' pagan gods. This was something strictly forbidden by God (Exodus 34:15–17; Deuteronomy 7:1–4). There is no doubt that this was a gradual thing. A little disobedience ends up in a lot of sin. By now, they were worshipping false gods, and they had lowered themselves to the immoral practices of these strange gods. The idols, Baal and Asherath, were known for this, as told in verse 7. Once again, as a result, the Lord was angry with them and He permitted the king of Syria to conquer them for eight years.

Following the cycle of sin, servitude, and repentance, we again see Israel crying out to the Lord. God in His great mercy gives them Caleb's nephew, Othniel, to save them. What a heritage he came from! Caleb was a man of great faith who God used to conquer the land. There is no doubt this rich and successful family background helped a man such as Othniel become a judge and deliverer for Israel. In verse 10, from the

Living Bible, we read, "The Spirit of the Lord took control of him and he reformed and purged Israel." This is the same phrase used in this same book about Gideon, Jepthah, and Samson. It is depictive of the special anointing of the Holy Spirit in the Old Testament. Certainly it shows that these men were more than mere political reformers. They were men specially used of God with the supernatural anointing of the Holy Ghost to bring victory to Israel.

Othniel's armies conquered the enemy and there was peace under his leadership for forty years until he died. Then, once again, the people turned away from God and resorted back to their old, sinful habits. And, once again, they were conquered and controlled by the enemy until the Lord raised up another judge. This time his name was Ehud, and he was a brave and mighty soldier who delivered Israel again and brought peace for the next eighty years. How exciting to see that the Lord always has someone to do His work, and that the Holy Spirit can make up for any shortages in our lives (Judges 3:31). God does not need us—we need God!

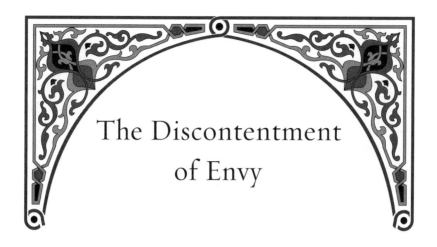

The Discontentment of Envy

RE: I Kings 21

As we have studied extensively the life of Ahab, and have seen the many idolatrous and wicked sins that he committed to dishonor and discredit God, it surely makes us wonder how God could put up with him for so long! In this lesson, we are about to discover the tragedy of something in Ahab's life that may seem relatively small in comparison to some of the other things he had done. However, it was the proverbial "straw to break the camel's back," and it brought judgment on him. The sin of envy will be the focus of attention in this lesson.

Let us take note of Exodus 20:17 (Living Bible), where God gave one of the commandments; "You must not be envious of your neighbor's house, or want to sleep with his wife, or want to own his slaves, oxen, donkeys, or anything else he has." Put simply, he said not to envy someone else's possessions. Envy comes when you resent the fact that others have what you don't. Resentment and envy go hand in hand. This is the case in I Kings 21 with King Ahab and a man called Naboth who had a vineyard on the outskirts of the city near King Ahab's palace. The king had approached Naboth to try to make a deal with him. First, he wanted to buy the land. Then he offered another piece of land in trade, in an attempt to persuade Naboth. Since the land was convenient to the palace,

Ahab wanted to make a palace garden. Naboth refused the king's offer, explaining, "This land has been in my family for generations."

Ahab returned to the palace angry and sullen. He was so upset about this that he refused to eat and went to bed "with his face to the wall." He actually went home to pout. Think about what you just read! The king went home to feel sorry for himself because he couldn't have what he wanted. Naboth was trying to uphold God's law, since it was considered a duty to keep ancestral land in the family. When Jezebel (Ahab's wicked wife) found out that Ahab was upset and angry, she wanted to know why. After Ahab told her what had happened, her evil mind went to work, planning a scheme that would eventually have Naboth killed.

She comforted Ahab, advising him to get up and eat, telling him not to worry because she was prepared to "handle" this situation. Jezebel then wrote letters in Ahab's name, sealed them with his seal, and addressed them to the civic leaders of Jezreel, where Naboth lived. In the letters she gave these instructions—"Call the citizens together for fasting and prayer. Then summon Naboth and find two scoundrels who will accuse him of cursing God and the king. Then take him out and execute him." The city fathers followed her instructions, assuming they came from her husband, the king. When Jezebel heard the news, she came to Ahab and told him, "You know the vineyard you wanted? You can have it now. Naboth is dead." So Ahab went to claim it. Envy and jealousy had driven these two wicked people to kill an innocent man just to get what they wanted.

Guess who then shows up? In obedience to the Spirit of God, Elijah, the prophet of God, comes on the scene. His words are fierce and filled with judgment; "I have come to place God's curse on you because you have sold yourself to the devil" (I Kings 21:20).

He then proceeds to recite God's punishment on Ahab and his household. "Because you have made God very angry and have led all Israel to sin. The Lord is going to bring great harm to you and your family. The dogs of Jezreel shall tear apart the body of your wife, and all the members of your family that die in the city. The dogs shall lick their blood, and those who die in the field shall be eaten of the vultures. Not a single male descendant will survive."

This was a tough prophecy, and understanding the voice of the prophet, Ahab heard it and put on sackcloth and ashes as a sign of repentance. God was so merciful that seeing Ahab's act of humility, He told Elijah that these things would not happen during his lifetime, but rather to his sons. All of this would come to pass as the Lord said, and we will see this more closely in further studies.

As we have seen, envy is a useless and detrimental emotion. If Ahab had only trusted God for everything, God would have given him the desire of his heart. Envy and jealousy uncorrected can lead to tragic results. Lord God, help us to humble ourselves before You, and seek first the kingdom of God, realizing that then and only then, all of these things shall be added unto us.

My dear brother or sister, we must wholeheartedly follow the Lord!

Deborah, a Woman of Confidence

RE: Judges 4; 5:19; Psalm 68:11

As we have already learned, because of their disobedience, the people of God were oppressed. They had little hope of ever winning a battle, but once again, our faithful God raised up a mighty leader: Deborah. Deborah knew her God would deliver His people if they would just obey Him.

The place where Israel fought the battle called "Midian" has the same root word as Armageddon. "Armageddon" signifies a place where man has done all he can do, therefore, God must act by divine intervention to bring victory.

In Judges 5:8, Israel's world fell apart when the people chose to follow false gods. Pressure from the outside became greater than power from within. Even though God had given Israel clear direction, the people had failed to put into practice the Word of the Lord. Instead, they lived on a false foundation of values that soon collapsed. They allowed a desire for recognition, a craving for power, and the love of money to rule their lives. When this happens, things may be good for a while, but eventually your world will fall apart around you.

In all of this, Deborah displayed a remarkable relationship with God. She had confidence that God would bring Israel out of its bondage and bring victory.

Her story shows that she was not power hungry. She only wanted to serve God. Whenever praise came her way, she gave God the credit. She did not deny or resist her position or her culture as a woman and wife, and she never allowed herself to be hindered by it either. Her story shows that God can accomplish great things through people who are willing to be led by Him, regardless of how it looks to man.

Deborah's life challenges us in several ways:

1. She reminds us of the need to be available both to God and to others.
2. She encourages us to use our efforts on what we can do rather than worrying about what we cannot do.
3. She challenges us to be wise leaders, using the abilities and talents of others.
4. She demonstrates what a person can accomplish when God is in control, even when circumstances do not live up to man's expectations.

Remember—God chooses leaders by His standards, not ours. Wise leaders choose good helpers.

A Mighty Man
of Valor—
Part I

RE: Judges 6

KEY VERSE: "As long as he sought the Lord, God made him to prosper" (2 Chronicles 26:5).

A pattern is commonly developed among people. When they forget the Lord, it always seems that things begin okay, but shortly thereafter, trouble begins. Judges 5:31 says, "There was peace in the land forty years," and Judges 6:1 continues, "Then the people began once again to worship other gods, and once again the Lord let their enemies harass them."

Imagine covenant people living under their privilege! Judges 6:2 tells us that the Israelites took to the mountains and had to live in caves and dens because of the strong hand of the Midianites. It was so bad that even when they planted crops, marauders from Midian, Amalek, and other surrounding nations came and destroyed their crops, leaving nothing to eat. They even stole their cattle, sheep, oxen, and donkeys. In fact, it says they completely stripped and devastated the land. Israel was reduced to abject poverty. Again, following the sin, servitude, and repentance cycle, at last the people began to cry out to the Lord for help.

God's reply was simple and direct through the prophet (notice that much of the prophet's words were not foretelling but forthtelling the mind of the Lord—declaring God's purpose and plan). God said several things to remind them of His faithfulness:

1. I brought you out of Egypt from slavery.
2. I rescued you from cruelty.
3. I drove out your enemies from before you.
4. I gave you their land.
5. I assured you I was your God.
6. I warned you not to worship false gods.
7. You have not listened to Me; you left Me—I never left you.

Notice, that even though God was terribly angry, He still displayed His mercy by revealing to Gideon that He was going to strengthen him for the work that He had for him to do.

God saw something in Gideon that He was going to use for His glory! The angel said, "Mighty Soldier, the Lord is with you!" Gideon had a few questions for the Lord:

1. If the Lord is with us, why are we in the condition we are in?
2. Where are all the miracles our ancestors told us about, such as when God brought us out of Egypt?
3. Why has He forsaken us and delivered us over to the Midianites?

The answer to all these questions was sin. God never leaves us; we leave Him (Leviticus 26; Deuteronomy 28). God said, "If you forsake Me and My Word, I will surrender you to your enemies." God has no choice but to allow you to make your own choices once you decide to step out of His will.

A Mighty Man
of Valor—
Part II

RE: Judges 6

The reason why Gideon had so many questions was simple. During his lifetime, he had heard much about what God did in the past, but he had not really seen anything happen. There are two truths here to consider:

1. We walk by faith, not by sight! (II Corinthians 5:7)
2. Sometimes people live on past blessings, but eventually, they become "bankrupt" and have to start over again.

It should be noted that almost 250 years had passed since the ten plagues and the parting of the Red Sea in Exodus 7–14. Two hundred years had passed since the last great miracle—the parting of the Jordan River in Joshua 3. Because of the lapse of time, Gideon wrongly assumed that God had given up on His people. Isn't it true that we always seem to want to judge God by what we think, rather than on God's character? Isn't it also true that we always seem to blame God for our troubles rather than examining ourselves? In this case, the people had given up on God. They knew what God expected of them. They had His laws. All they had to do was to trust God! All we have to do is trust His Word—He will take care of the rest!

In Ezekiel 22:30, God says, "I am sending you." When God says, in Judges 6:14, "I am sending you," it is obvious that He becomes the provider! He says, "I will make you strong!" (I Peter 5:10; Philippians 4:13). Gideon begins to make excuses, saying, "My family is the poorest in the whole tribe of Manasseh, and I am the least thought of in the entire family." In other words, "I can't!"

Notice what God says in Judges 6:14 (Living Bible); "But, I Jehovah, will be with you! And you shall quickly destroy the Midianite hordes." And notice these words, "But, I Jehovah," (It literally says), "I am, will be with you." The same name is used here as in Exodus 3:14. God is telling Gideon that the same one who appeared to Moses and rescued Israel from Egypt will be with him (which, by the way, was heavily on Gideon's mind, as we can see from verse 13).

In Exodus 3, review Moses' experience, and notice that God keeps saying "I" and Moses keeps saying, how am I going to do it? Reminding God of our limitations implies that He does not know all about us or that He is making a mistake in evaluating our character.

Remember, the Bible says, "Man looketh on the outward appearance, but God looketh on the heart."

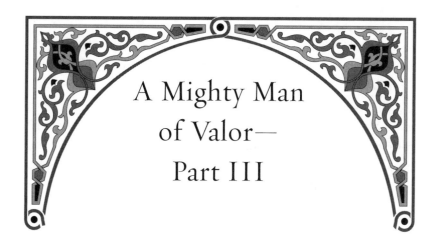

A Mighty Man
of Valor—
Part III

RE: Judges 6

God will always confirm His Word to His servants. Just like in Gideon's case, God always knows the person He chooses is capable of the task chosen. The angel of the Lord appeared to Gideon to give him a sign. In fact, before the job was done, there were four signs:

1. Miraculous consumption of the food (Judges 6:21).
2. Dew only on the fleece, not on the floor where the fleece lay (Judges 6:37, 38).
3. Dew only on the floor, not on the fleece (Judges 6:39, 40).
4. Dream of the barley cake falling in the midst of Midian (Judges 7:9–15).

God will reply to our request, if we are willing to reply to His. What did He ask? Let's examine this.

First, we see that after the angel appeared, Gideon thought he was going to die (this was tradition). It is interesting to see what he did. After the angel said, "Peace be unto you, thou shalt not die," we find out in Judges 6:24 what he did; "Then Gideon built an altar there unto the Lord." Notice that Gideon was not commanded to do this. He did this as an act of worship to the Lord. He called it "Jehovah-Shalom," the literal translation being "the God of Peace." It really states "peace in the struggle!"

In any battle or struggle of life, we must know that God's peace will keep us (Philippians 4:7; Colossians 3:15; Ephesians 4:12). After his own private altar is established to God, he is ready to begin the battle. Before any military strategy is employed, there is yet another job to do—tear down the false altar! Here are God's commands in Judges 6: 25, 26:

1. Take the best of your father's bullock.
2. Throw down the altar of Baal that your father set up.
3. Cut down the grove by the altar.
4. Build an altar to Jehovah.
5. Offer the bullock upon the altar.

This signifies what is always the first step back to God—repentance, getting rid of anything you know restricts or hinders you, and then continuing on with God. Not everyone was happy. The people wanted to kill Gideon, and many of them were fellow Israelites. Just think of how sinful they had become. God said in Deuteronomy 13:6–11 that idolaters must be stoned to death. Here, they wanted to stone Gideon!

Out of this comes an interesting name for Gideon—Jerubbaal. The meaning of this is "Shame on Baal!" We could translate this, "Shame on the Devil," or, "Devil killer" (Judges 6:32).

It should be noted that as a result of Gideon's steps, we read, "The Spirit of the Lord came upon Gideon." A visible anointing clothed him.

When we take the necessary steps to prepare ourselves, God will do His part to meet us. The anointing of the Holy Spirit will be enough for us to defeat the enemy. Even though Gideon could sense this anointing, he still needed another sign from the Lord, and he received two. Sometimes we ask, "Why?" Remember, Old Testament people did not have the Holy Spirit in them, and they did not have the New Testament. They had to have God cause different things to happen because His physical presence was their only source. We don't have to put fleeces out as Gideon did. A fleece should never substitute the wisdom of God that comes through studying the Bible and Bible-based prayer.

Gideon did not have the two most valuable things that we possess: the Holy Spirit in us and the written Word of God to guide us. One of our greatest commands is II Timothy 2:15, which says, "Study to show thyself approved unto God, a workman that needeth not be ashamed, rightly dividing the Word of truth." Demanding extra signs was an indication of unbelief. Fear often causes us to look for more confirmation, when what is needed is our simple obedience. Visible signs are unnecessary if they are only confirming what we already know is true (1 Corinthians 1:22–25).

Gideon was now about to learn a valuable lesson. When God calls and we say yes, it is going to require us to follow *His* plan. Where God guides—God provides! In this case, God tells Gideon something that I don't think he wanted to hear.

Gideon had sent word out to all the surrounding territories to round up the troops (Judges 6:35). It says they all responded. Now, in Judges 7:2, God says, "There are too many of you! If I let all of you fight the Midianites, you will boast that you saved yourselves by your own strength." So God says, "Send home all the timid and frightened." As a result, 22,000 of them picked up their things, leaving only 10,000 remaining to fight the battle. That was a great number that left, but God says, "You still have too many." He tells Gideon to bring the remaining 10,000 to the river to test them. If the soldiers lap water from their hands, as a dog watches for an enemy, they may remain, but if they kneel to drink in the river, carelessly, they are to be rejected and told to go home. Only 300 men pass the test. They are about to face an army of over 135,000! With an army this small, there would be no doubt that any victory would be from God!

The truth to learn here is, like Gideon, we must recognize the danger of fighting in our own strength. We can only be confident of victory if we put our trust in God and not in ourselves. Without Him we can do nothing, but with Him, we can do all things! (Proverbs 3: 5–7; Psalm 127:1)

Remember the words of the Lord in Judges 7:7; "I'll conquer the Midianites with these 300."

During the night, God awakens Gideon and tells him to take his troops and attack the Midianites. (We know from Judges 8:10 that there had to be at least 135,000 in the Midianite army.) God tells Gideon, "I will cause you to defeat them"; this should have been obvious, because it was impossible in their own strength!

Note the loving kindness of our God! He says, "If you are afraid, first go down to the camp alone—take your servant Purah—and listen to what they are saying down there."

Facing overwhelming odds, Gideon was afraid. God understood his fear, but He did not excuse him from his task. In the midst of the battle, God still comforts us and confirms His Word.

Notice in Judges 7: 13–15 how the text describes the number of troops in the valley; it says they are "like locusts, sand on the seashore." Isn't it amazing that God brings Gideon and Purah to the right tent? In the middle of the night, a man awakens, perhaps thinking he was having a nightmare, and Gideon and Purah are hiding outside the tent. They hear the man telling his roommate about his dream of a huge loaf of barley bread that came tumbling down into their camp. "It hit our tent," he explains, "and knocked it flat!" The other soldier replied, "Your dream can mean only one thing! Gideon, the son of Joash, the Israelite, is going to come and massacre all the allied forces of Midian." Barley grain was only half the value of wheat, and the bread made from it was considered inferior. Comparatively, Israel's tiny band of men was considered inferior to the vast forces of Midian and Amalek.

What would the odds be for Gideon to show up at a tent in the middle of 135,000 soldiers where he would overhear such a testimony? God always has everything under control! They that put their trust in the Lord shall never be ashamed! When Gideon heard the men in the tent, he could only stand there and worship God. When he returned, he aroused the troops and was ready to see God do all that He had promised.

Constantly Follow God!

RE: Judges 8

Key Lesson: Even those who make great spiritual progress can easily fall into sin if they do not consistently follow God (I Corinthians 15:56; Ecclesiastes 9:11; Philippians 3:12–15).

The lesson to learn from Gideon is really simple, but the responsibility is complex. Most of us suffer not from what we don't know, but what we know and don't do. Gideon had learned that "little is much when God is in it" (Remember, of course, the reduction of an army to 300). He also learned that God is very capable of helping us to overcome natural difficulties. Review three significant facts about his life:

1. His family background (Judges 6:15)
2. His personal inadequacies (Judges 6:15)
3. His doubts about his call (Judges 6:17)

Gideon was going to discover that God uses common people who are dedicated to Him. Below are some notable examples:

Jephthah: The son of a prostitute—God used him to deliver Israel from the Amorites (Judges 11).

David: A shepherd boy and last born of his family—used to become Israel's greatest king (I Samuel 16).

Esther: A slave girl—used to save her people from massacre (Esther).

Moses: A shepherd and murderer in exile—used to deliver Israel out of Egypt and lead them into the Promised Land (Exodus 3).

Jacob: A liar and supplanter—used to father the Israelite nation (Genesis 27).

Amos: A fruit picker—used as a prophet to God's people (Amos).

It is very important to notice that Gideon was a great military leader and was used to restore Israel to peace for forty years (Judges 8:28). Mistakenly, the people wanted him to be a king over them, but Gideon refused, saying, "The Lord will rule over you, He is your king." Even though he made that great statement, his following statement perhaps became a great snare to his life. He said that he had one request. He wanted all the earrings collected from their fallen foes. Gideon had them melted them down and made a golden ephod, which was a robe worn by a priest. The people worshipped it and made it like a god, prostituting themselves. Gideon also fathered a son, Abimelech, from a sexual relationship out of marriage, and Abimelech became a snare to Israel.

Make a note of the three critical sins of Gideon:

1. He collected Midianite gold to make a golden ephod.
2. He produced a son (Abimelech) from a sexual relationship outside of marriage.
3. He failed to train his family in God's ways and after he died, they all went back to idol worship.

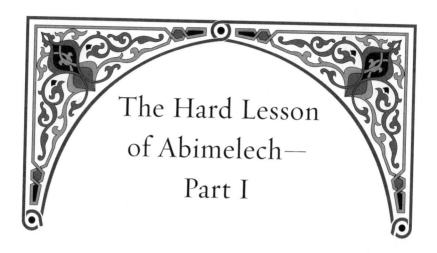

The Hard Lesson of Abimelech— Part I

Gideon (Abimilech's father) succeeded in military battles, but sometimes failed in his personal struggles. Gideon was not condemned for taking a concubine (Judges 8:31), but the family problems that resulted from his son born out of this relationship are clearly stated in this chapter.

When Gideon died, Abimelech wanted to take his father's place as king. To set his plan in motion, to get what he wanted, he went to the city of Shechem (his mother's hometown) to drum up support. Here he felt close kinship with the residents, since this is where he came from (he used this issue to gain recognition). Shortly thereafter, Abimelech felt confident he had enough support and he was declared king. "He is our brother," the people reasoned, "a local native."

Israel's king was to be the Lord, not a man; however, Israel continued to refuse to accept God's plan. Let's review Gideon's words in Judges 8:23, 24; "I will not be your king, nor shall my son: the Lord is your King." Gideon had already clearly stated neither he, nor his sons, would be king, but Abimelech was very selfish.

First of all, we find that he had surrounded himself with the wrong kind of people. He accepted money offered to idols and perhaps procured through temple prostitution. He also used the money to hire "worthless loafers" (LB), also known as "vain and light persons" (KJV). Proverbs 12:11 says, "He that followeth vain persons is void of understanding."

People with selfish ambitions often seek to fulfill them in ruthless ways. In his selfish quest, he killed all but one of his seventy (that's right, seventy) brothers. Jotham was the only one who escaped—and it was Jotham who publicly denounced his half brother, Abimelech, by prophesying about him through a parable. He actually told them that if they wanted God's blessing, they should not follow Abimelech. He went on to explain that if they did, in the end they would all be destroyed. The Bible says, "Fools make a mock at sin."

It took three years for this prophecy to take place, but just as Jotham had said, it came to pass. The text is very interesting. The KJV says, "God sent an evil spirit between Abimelech and the people of Shechem" (I Samuel 16:14; I Kings 12:15). I Kings 18:19 in the Living Bible says, "God stirred up trouble," or, caused trouble to stir up between them. God knows how to straighten us out. Abimelech had three years to change his ways. God would have forgiven him. Please understand that all prophecy is conditional. Do you remember Nebuchadnezzar-Belshazzar? If we will not do what God wants, God will do what He wants. God was not going to let Abimelech escape without repenting. A man who refuses to admit his mistakes can never be successful. If he repents and confesses his mistakes, he then gets another chance. The Bible says, "Be sure your sins will find you out."

God is not a fool, and He is not mocked. He is God, even if we fail to recognize Him for who He is!

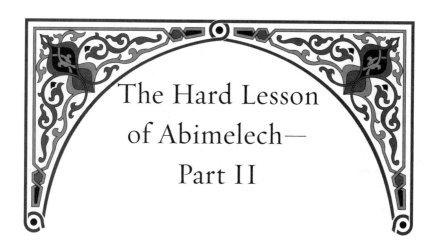

The Hard Lesson of Abimelech— Part II

RE: Judges 9

We have found that where there is no repentance, the judgment of sin will ensue and may very well carry over to the next generation. God is quick to forgive when there is repentance. Abimelech refused to do so. In fact, God intervened to make sure he would be punished for his insolence.

Rebellion rose up against Abimelech. He discovered that the same people who promoted him to office were suddenly against him. A civil war emerged, and there was much bloodshed. Abimelech was a very shrewd military leader, so he was able to defeat many of his enemies. However, it should be noted that God was literally getting back at him and the people of Shechem. Abimelech was killing people, and God was getting ready to punish him—and punish him He did. Abimelech went to the city of Thebez, encamped against them, and took it. There was a fort and strong tower in the city, and all of the people ran to the rooftop for protection. Abimelech approached the tower to burn it, but a woman standing atop of the tower threw a millstone upon his head and crushed his skull. In fact, it was utterly embarrassing that a woman would have been known to be the one who killed him, so he asked one of his soldiers to draw his sword and kill him so no one would know that a woman killed him! (Judges 9:50–57)

What a shame—a young man who had such a godly father turned out so terrible! One of the lessons to learn from Abimelech is that our goals control our actions. The amount of control is related to the importance of the goal. Abimelech's most prominent goal and intention was to have power. His lust for power drove him to murder his own family. The contrast between Abimelech and other great people in Scripture is that Abimelech wanted power to control, while great men and women of God want to be controlled by God. The Holy Spirit in us leads, guides, and directs us—but in direct contrast, a person led by the Devil is driven, forced, and compelled to do the things they do.

Proverbs 28:10 says, "Only a stupid prince will oppress his people, but a king will have long reign if he hates dishonesty and bribes."

Proverbs 18:12 says, "Pride ends in destruction, humility ends in honor."

The key verse, for our purposes, is Judges 9:56, which says, "Thus God punished Abimelech and the men of Shechem for their sin of murdering Gideon's seventy sons."

The lesson is very simple—following God means forsaking all! Selfish motives always result in falling away from God's plan for our lives. Even though God's mercy gives us chance after chance, we must still obey His word or suffer the consequences (Proverbs 1:28, 29).

Judges 9:57 is God's ultimate punishment. It says, "And all the evil of the men of Shechem did God render upon their heads: and upon them came the curse of Jotham the son of Jerubbaal."

Sin is not worth it!

Restoration, Again

RE: *Judges* 10

In the first five verses, we read about two judges: Tola and Jair. Notably, the Scripture records nothing about them other than they lived and died. What are we doing for God that is worth noting? When our life is over, will people remember more than just the number of years we have lived?

A recurring problem is repeated in Judges 10:6. Israel turned away from the Lord again, and worshipped the heathen gods Baal and Ashtaroth, and the gods of Syria, Sidon, Moab, Amnon, and Philistia. The Living Bible says, "Not only this, but they no longer worshipped Jehovah at all." The KJV says bluntly, " They forsook the Lord." One of the reasons why there were so many false gods is explained in Psalm 106:34–36. It says that they did not destroy the nations in the land as God told them to, but "mingled" among the heathen and learned their evil ways. We must guard our hearts with all diligence. We must come out from among them and be separate! This whole scene went on for eighteen years until finally, the Israelites turned to Jehovah, and begged Him to save them, confessing that they had sinned. Sin, servitude, and repentance once again.

God was always ready to forgive them as they confessed before Him, but He reminded them of all the times in the past that He was there to help them. He now tells them in verse 14, "Go cry to the new gods you have chosen! Let them save you in your hour of distress!" (Psalm 106:43; I John 2:2).

We see here how good our God is all of the time. He is a very present help in the time of trouble. He hears their cry for help and sees them in their utter misery. They became so miserable that they were willing to fall into God's just and punishing hands rather than suffer at the hands of their enemy. Notice they said, "Punish us in any way you see fit," only save us from our enemies (Judges 10:15).

While this was a noble prayer, it was not enough. We must bring forth fruit "meet for repentance" (Judges 10:16). Realizing this, they destroyed their foreign gods and worshipped only the Lord. If there is anything that gets God's attention, it is when we worship Him! Notice that the Bible says God was grieved by their misery. God was ready to begin the restoration process once again! He is just and true, and always patient with us. While the armies of Ammon were ready to attack Israel, God, the Master Strategist, was preparing for victory! (II Chronicles 7:14; Joshua 24:23, 24; Jeremiah 18:7, 8)

God Uses Us in Spite of Us, Not Because of Us

RE: Judges 11

KEY VERSE: "So Jepthah led his armies against the Ammonites and the Lord gave him the victory" (Judges 11:32).

We found out that the Israelites seemed to forget God when things were going well. Even though rejected by His people, God never failed to rescue them when they sincerely cried out to Him. We should understand that when we reject or ignore God, He feels similar to the way a parent feels when a child rebels or disobeys. We must stay close to God and not run the risk of allowing sin to run rampant in us, thus alienating ourselves from God and placing ourselves into His judgment (I Samuel 8:7).

The Israelites had a great task on their hands. The Ammonites (descendants of Lot through incest with his daughter) were at the peak of their power. It would take a mighty warrior to still the enemy. That man's name would be Jepthah. He was a great warrior from the land of Gilead. As is the case so often in the Word of God, God chose to use a person who did not necessarily have a "good reputation." Jepthah was born to a prostitute, and the Living Bible bluntly describes him as "a son of a whore." Would you agree that is an auspicious debut in the pages of Bible history? His half brothers decided to force him out of their father's estate, so Jepthah fled to a far away place. Actually, this young man was suffering from his parent's sinful decisions, and not for any wrong that he had done. Yet, in spite of his brother's rejection, God used him. If you have suffered or are suffering from an unfair rejection, don't blame others and become bitter or discouraged. Remember how God used Jepthah, despite his unjust circumstances, and realize that He is able and willing to use you, despite the natural circumstances!

Circumstances beyond Jepthah's control forced him to run away as a social outcast. Great potential was also wasted because of prejudice. Jepthah is listed as a "faith hero" in Hebrews 11:32. His story is one of faith. We know a lot of things about this man from Scripture. One thing that we see about him is that although he was a rough, tough man (verse 29), "The Spirit of the Lord came upon him." God is the only one that can judge the heart (Remember David's anointing to be king.). With all the judges in Israel, this was the only one who ever stated that Jehovah was the people's real, true judge. Judges 11:27 reveals to us that God does not bless us because of us, but in spite of us. We, in and of ourselves, are nothing, and there is nothing we could ever do to deserve or earn the blessing of God.

Judges 13 shows that every judge brought a measure of deliverance and peace to Israel. We can note the difference between people who have strong leadership and those who do not. After the death of each judge, since Israel could not withstand their enemies without a strong leader, they would fall back into bondage. Remember, it was God's command that the law was to be deposited not only in the leader's mouth, but to be passed down to his children and great-grandchildren, so that the heritage of God's Word would be carried out (Isaiah 59:21) (This is also repeated in Deuteronomy).

One of the interesting things about our God is that He never gives up on us, even though we are ready to give up on Him. We see this so clearly as we begin Judges 13. Once again, the people had turned to the cycle of sin and servitude, and were in need of repentance. Notice also, as they turned to worship other gods, the Lord allowed them to be conquered by the Philistines. This is the law of cause and effect that God has set into motion. They turned with their own free will, and God let them be conquered by the Philistines. For forty years they were subjected to bondage that they brought upon themselves. God did not cause His people to suffer. It was a result of the people ignoring God, and He allowed it.

Judges 10:18 says, "Whoever volunteers shall be our king." Jepthah was the man. Here, in Judges 13, there were no volunteers. God was sovereignly choosing one. By divine intervention, he dispatched the angel of the Lord to a woman who had no children and her husband Manoah. It never ceases to amaze me that in the middle of total national degradation and sin, there are still people who are capable of hearing from God! The angel gave specific instructions. He declared to her that she was going to have a baby boy and explained that she would have to raise him as a Nazarite. There were four conditions for a Nazarite:

1. No alcohol
2. No cutting of hair
3. No touching dead
4. No eating of unclean food

This vow that the Nazarite took was to set him apart for God's service for life. There are no recourses for a call from God. When God calls, we have no alternative but to respond with a lifetime service. The gifts and callings of God are without repentance. This is not a temporary call that we can get out of any time we want. We are to be witnesses of what God has called us to (Examples to study: Moses, Elijah, John).

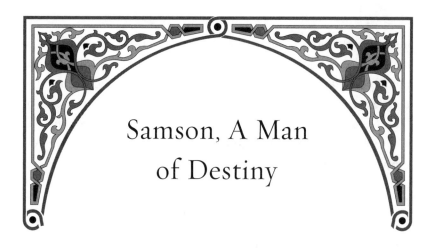

Samson, A Man of Destiny

RE: Judges 13–15; Hebrews 11:32

From the time of a prophetic announcement, Samson was going to be a key figure in God's deliverance for Israel from the Philistine enemy. Remember that Samson had a divine beginning by the angel of the Lord predicting his birth and giving instruction on how he was to control his life and his divine destiny. Judges 13:5 declares, "He will begin to rescue Israel from the Philistines."

How wonderful it is to see parents such as Samson's, so dedicated to the Lord (much like Samuel's parents). They were sensitive enough to hear God's voice through the angel of the Lord, and had enough faith to believe what had been spoken. At the command of the angel, they offered a grain offering to the Lord (symbolic of honor, respect, and worship to God in Leviticus 2). It was an acknowledgement to God for His provision. By this, Manoah was showing his desire to serve God and demonstrated his respect. "Train up a child in the way he should go, and when he is old he will not depart from it." Obeying the angel's command to keep Samson as a Nazarite from birth, Samson's parents protected God's divine call upon his life.

Even as a young man, Samson began to realize his destiny. Note that in Judges 13:25, while hanging around his warlike tribe of Dan, he felt the yearnings of war to establish a permanent and settled territory. It is important to note that time spent in preparation is very important to the overall success of what God desires to do in our lives. It was here at military headquarters that God used divine intervention and caused the Holy Spirit to move on him. This was Samson's first real experience of Holy Ghost power, and it would be repeated a few more times in his life. The more we study the life of Samson, the more we see a man who was supernaturally prepared for his task by God. It will become clearer and clearer that it could not have been human strength or ability. It had to be God working on his behalf.

Mark 16:20 says, "And they went, forth, and preached everywhere, the Lord working with them, and confirming the word with signs following."

As we see in Judges 14 and Hebrews 11:32, it is sad to be remembered for what we might have been. Samson had tremendous potential. Not many people have started life as he did. Born as a result of God's plan in the lives of Manoah and his wife, Samson was to be "a special servant of God." He was to begin to rescue Israel from the Philistines. His life shows us that even when God thoroughly equips us, we still must do what is at hand to do to make certain that we do not forfeit God's ultimate plan for our lives (II Peter 1:8–10).

On many occasions, Samson violated both his Nazarite vow and God's laws. His life was controlled by desires that would often cause him to lose sight of his primary reason for life—serving God and His people. We must remember that although Samson possessed a great ability to exercise physical feats, his ability did not come from physical strength.

In Judges 13:25; 14:6; 14:19; and 15:14, we read, "The Spirit of the Lord came upon him." In fact, his physical appearance couldn't have shown him to be strongly built, because the Philistines had to use Delilah to find out where he got his strength! Often when discussing Samson's life, people forget that it is God's equipping that establishes us, as it did Samson.

We also see that Samson would often use the gifts God placed in his hands impulsively and for selfish purposes. The gifts that God gives are given to edify the body—to bring the body to a position of strength and maturity, not for our own gain (Ephesians 4:12).

Samson was set apart for special service to God from birth; but for the most part, he ignored his vow of devotion, depending more and more on his ability rather than on God's. This was a crucial mistake.

Valuable lessons to be learned:

1. Being strong in God in one area does not make up for weaknesses in other areas. We must strive to be strong in Him in every area of life.

2. God's presence will never supercede a person's will.

3. Samson's life proves that no matter how low a person has stooped, he can still recover from what appears to be utter failure.

Dealing With Critical Circumstances

RE: Ruth 1

The story of Ruth takes place sometime during the period of the judges. These were dark days for Israel. Everyone did whatever seemed "right in his own eyes." Unfortunately, perversion and moral depravity were the rule, not the exception. But in the midst of those dark and evil times, there were still some who followed God. The book of Ruth tells of two such people—Ruth and Naomi. They were a beautiful picture of loyalty, friendship, and commitment to God and each other. This book also shows how people remained strong in character and true to God even when the society around them was collapsing. As we briefly trace the steps of these two women, we will see God's faithfulness to man's loyalty.

In the beginning of the book, we find Elimelech, a Jew, moving his whole family to Moab. This is really strange in the sense that Moab was one of Israel's oppressors during the period of the judges (Judges 3:12). However, the famine in Israel must have been so severe that Elimelech had no choice but to take his wife, Naomi, and their two sons to Moab. It should be noted that friendly relations with Moabites were discouraged, but not forbidden (Deuteronomy 23:6). Marrying a Canaanite, however, was against God's laws (Deuteronomy 7:3). Moabites were not allowed to worship at the temple because they had refused to let the Israelites pass through their land when exiting Egypt. Ironically, as God's chosen nation, Israel should have set high standards of moral living for other nations, yet it was Ruth, a Moabite, whom God used as an example of genuine spiritual character.

Shortly after Elimelech and his family arrived in Moab, he died. His two sons married Orpah and Ruth, but the sons died also. Naomi was left alone with Orpah and Ruth. Naomi told her daughters-in-law that they were returning to Israel, because she heard that there were good crops in the land once again. On the journey, she told both daughters-in-law to go back to Moab, because they were not obligated to go with her to Israel. She also explained that they would be able to marry there among their own kind.

An interesting verse here is Ruth 1:8 in the Living Bible, "May the Lord reward you for your faithfulness to your husbands and to me." It was a hopeless, helpless situation to be a widow stranded in the ancient world. Most widows were ignored and poverty stricken. The law provided that the nearest relative would take care of them. However, since Naomi did not know if any relatives lived in Israel, it was really hopeless. Yet her unselfish attitude made her willing to send her daughters-in-law back home to get on with their lives.

As they were saying their goodbyes, Ruth insisted that she could not leave Naomi. Her most famous words are in chapter 1, verse 16, and they display the intensity of her loyalty to Naomi and her faithfulness to God, "Your people shall be my people, your God my God." Ruth was now committed to Naomi to go wherever she would go.

We then see them returning to Bethlehem. It was spring and time to harvest barley. Naomi had experienced severe hardship. She was returning home widowed and poor. She decided to change her name from Naomi (pleasant) to Mara (bitter). She expresses great pain, bitterness, and disappointment. Sometimes in our bitterness and disappointment, we forget that God is still on the throne and has everything under control!

In Ruth 2:1 and 2, we find Ruth ready to go out into the field to glean. When the reapers went out to cut barley, they would tie the stalks in the field in bundles. Israelite law demanded that the corners of the fields not be harvested. In addition, any grain that was dropped was also to be left for the gleaners (poor people who were free to pick up the left-over grain). The purpose of this law was to provide food for the poor and prevent the owners from hoarding. This law served as a type of "welfare" program in Israel (Leviticus 19:9; 23:22; Deuteronomy 24:19). This is why we see Ruth gleaning in the field. Notice that she was not in just any field. Naomi's in-law, Boaz, was the owner of the field. God was getting ready to do something supernatural and very exciting.

In God's Kingdom There Are No Accidents

RE: Ruth 1, 2

Many times our lives are filled with turmoil because we are constantly trying to find God's will for our lives. Sometimes the harder we try, the worse our turmoil becomes. The reason for this is that, with no regard for anything else, we attempt to find God's will. By this I mean that we must pursue God's Word for His general will before He will begin to reveal anything else to us.

Ruth was not an ordinary person. Given the choice of choosing her own way of life soon after the death of her husband, she chose not to accompany her widowed sister-in-law, Orpah, who returned to her own homeland. Realizing she was now a virtually helpless widow, Ruth's choice was to be loyal and faithful to her mother-in-law, Naomi.

We find her back at Naomi's hometown, Bethlehem, out in the field God specifically, by Divine Providence, sets her up to be in—Boaz's field, Naomi's in-law! This is no accident! Notice how the writer states it in Ruth 2:3—"As it happened" (Living Bible), and, "And her hap" (KJV).

There are no accidents to those who walk upright before God. The Bible says, "The steps of a righteous man are ordered by the Lord, and he delighteth in his way." God was getting ready to honor Ruth's faith and dedication to Naomi. When we are allowing our steps to be ordered by

God, we end up in the right place at the right time, and we are literally setting ourselves up for God's blessing to come upon our lives.

A field foreman told Boaz that the young lady he had noticed in the field gleaning was the young lady who had recently accompanied her mother-in-law back from Moab. She was working hard in the fields, gathering up anything left behind by the reapers.

Boaz began to talk to her and invited her to join the others in rest and refreshment. He even invited her to lunch—an unusual event for a gleaner. Ruth went back to Naomi and told her everything that happened.

A divine encounter had unfolded.

The Closer I Walk, The Better I Know

RE: Ruth 2

One of the more interesting verses in Scripture, concerning the story of Ruth, is found in Ruth 2:10–12. Foreigners were not always welcomed in Israel, but Boaz gladly welcomed Ruth, because she had gained a reputation for showing kindness and generosity to others. Ruth's past actions were a "report card" by which others judged her. Her good reputation was her most valuable asset. It came as a result of her hard work, strong moral character, and the sensitivity, kindness, and loyalty she easily displayed to Naomi. A good reputation is built upon godly character and kindness towards others. Ruth was consistently loyal and faithful to Naomi. Inconsistent with Israeli law, Boaz pronounced blessings on Ruth and provided protection and personal blessing to her while she gleaned. This godly character in Ruth was going to set up Boaz to make a very important decision concerning Naomi's house and the carrying on of the family name.

Though Ruth may not have always recognized God's guidance in her life, He had been with her every step of the way. She went to glean and "just happened" to end up in the field owned by Boaz who "just happened" to be a close relative of Naomi's husband. This was more than mere coincidence! God was at work in the entire situation!

As we go about our daily tasks, we should also have the confidence that God is at work in our lives. Many times, He is at work in our lives in ways we cannot even recognize. We must not close the door to what God can do. For the believer, events do not occur through luck or coincidence. We have faith that God is directing our lives for His purpose. Psalm 23:6 declares, "Surely, goodness and mercy shall follow me all the days of my life."

If we are walking in God's will, we are constantly being tracked down by goodness and mercy. Hosea 6:3 says, "Then shall we know, if we follow on to know the Lord: his going forth is prepared as the morning; and he shall come unto us as the rain, as the latter and former rain unto the earth."

The closer we walk with God, the better we know Him. His voice becomes clearer and clearer, and the things He requires of us become easier and easier to do. We must live righteously, by studying His Word, fellowshipping with Him, and getting to know Him better. Then, surely, He will order our steps.

Divine Arrangement

RE: Ruth 3

Ruth 3:1 says, "One day Naomi said to Ruth, 'My dear, isn't it time that I try to find a husband for you, and get you happily married again?'"

As widows, Ruth and Naomi could only foresee difficult times. But when Naomi heard the news about Boaz, and that Ruth was indeed working in the field of her family (Ruth 2:20), it renewed her hope and faith. Typical of Naomi's character, she thought first of Ruth. She encouraged her to see if Boaz would take the responsibility of being a "kinsman-redeemer" to her.

A kinsman-redeemer was a relative who volunteered to take responsibility for the extended family. Because Ruth's husband had died, the law in Deuteronomy 25:5–10 provided that she could marry a brother of the dead husband (one of Naomi's sons). The only problem was that Naomi had no more sons, so, in that case, the nearest relative to Ruth's husband could become a kinsman-redeemer and marry Ruth. The nearest relative did not have to marry the widow. If he chose not to, the next nearest relative could take his place. If no one chose to help the widow, she would probably live in poverty the rest of her life. In Israelite culture, the inheritance was only passed on to the son or nearest male relative, not to the wife. To take the sting out of these inheritance rules, there were laws for gleaning and kinsman-redeemers.

We have a kinsman-redeemer in Jesus Christ, who, though He was God, came to earth as a man in order to save us. By His death on the cross, He has redeemed us from sin and hopelessness, thereby purchasing us to be His own possession (I Peter 1:18, 19). Glory to God!

Naomi's plan to have Ruth go to Boaz was very successful. Boaz was an unselfish man. He could have easily rejected any request from a woman like Ruth, a Moabite (foreigner), in a society where even local Israelite women were regarded more as property than anything else. He was indeed very kind and loving to her request. There was one more step to take before he could become kinsman-redeemer; Boaz was not the nearest relative, so the nearest relative would first have to be contacted. The nearest relative could be found at the entrance gate to the city. When he was found, he refused to accept Ruth because then he would have to give equal share of his inheritance to Ruth's sons, and he was unwilling. Now, Boaz could have what he wanted and take Ruth as his bride. Ruth was not aware that the larger choices made in her life would one day set her in a place to become a part of the lineage of Jesus (Ruth 4:15; Matthew 1:1–5).

Prepare today so that tomorrow you will look back at the handiwork of God in your life, just as Ruth did.

Cross the Finish Line

RE: I Samuel 1

In the book of I Samuel, we find several important things, including: the record of the life of Samuel, Israel's last judge; the reign and decline of Saul, the first king; and the choice and preparation of David, Israel's greatest king.

The book begins in the days of the judges and describes Israel's transition from a theocracy (led by God) to a monarchy (led by a king). It is so sad that I Samuel is a book of great beginnings and tragic endings, as we will study. It begins with Eli as high priest during the time of the judges.

As a religious leader, Eli certainly must have begun his life in close communication with God. In his communication with Hannah and the training of her son, Samuel, Eli demonstrated a clear understanding of God's purpose and call (chapters 1 and 3). His life ended in disgrace as God judged his sacrilegious sons and the sacred ark of the covenant fell into enemy hands (chapter 4). Eli's death marked the decline of the high priest and the rise of the prophet in Israel.

In any race, although the start is important, the finish is more crucial. Often a frontrunner will lose strength and fade into the middle of the pack. Then there is the tragedy of the brilliant beginner who sets the pace and keeps it for a time, but does not finish. He quits the race, burned out, exhausted, or injured. This seems to be repeated over and over in I Samuel. The main characters of the story are Eli, Samuel, and Saul, but it is not foreign to our days, or New Testament days. Hear the heart's cry of the Apostle Paul, in II Timothy 4:10, 11, as he talks of those who started with him but are now long gone from him. Hear the heart cry of John the Revelator as the Spirit through Him urges the church of Philadelphia to "hold fast," or, hold tightly to what you have (Revelation 3:10, 11).

Paul's exhortation to Timothy in II Timothy 4:7 in the Living Bible is, "I have fought long and hard for my Lord, and through it all I have kept true to him." The King James Version says, "I have fought a good fight, I have finished the course." What a statement! We too, must press on to the high calling of God in Christ Jesus. Like a runner in a race, we must keep a steady pace and remain undistracted by the bad and the good that happens throughout the course.

Divine Birth

RE: I Samuel 1

The book of I Samuel begins in the days when the judges still ruled Israel, possibly during the closing days of Samson's life. It begins with what we might consider a miracle intervention by God concerning the birth of Samuel. He was going to make quite an impact on Israel by being qualified as a judge and priest, after having grown up under the spiritual leadership of Eli. It is clear from reading the first three chapters of I Samuel that God was preparing him to lead the nation. He became the first and last judge to serve as both priest and prophet. He was a great example of a good judge by governing the people by God's Word and not his own impulses. Let's look at his sovereign birth.

Jeremiah 1:5 says, "I knew you before you were formed within your mother's womb; before you were born I sanctified you and appointed you as my spokesman to the world." If this was true of Jeremiah, and God does not change, then it was surely true of Samuel, as it is for us today.

The tabernacle was located in Shiloh, the religious center of the nation (I Samuel 1:3). Three times a year, all the Israelite men were required to attend a religious feast held at the tabernacle. The feasts were: Passover, The Feast of Shelters, and The Feast of Weeks (Deuteronomy 16:16). Elkanah, Samuel's father, made his pilgrimage regularly to fulfill God's command. Hannah, Samuel's mother, had been unable to conceive. In Old Testament times, barrenness was thought to be failure on the part of the woman. Her barrenness was a social embarrassment to her husband. Although Elkanah could have left Hannah because a husband was permitted to divorce a barren wife, he remained lovingly devoted to her, despite social criticism and his rights under civil law.

Peninah, Elkanah's other wife, would continuously mock and jeer Hannah. Although polygamy existed and was permitted, it was never ordained of God and would often cause division and strife, as in I Samuel 1:7. Elkanah still loved Hannah and would encourage her. By supporting those who are struggling with comfort and edification, we may be helping them to remain strong enough in God to remain in obedience and confidence in Him, allowing us to see His ultimate plan unfold in their lives.

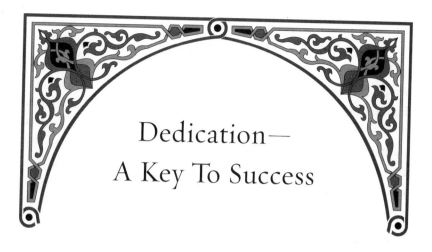

Dedication—
A Key To Success

RE: I Samuel 1, 2

The exciting and interesting thing about Hannah and Elkanah was that during a time when many people in the land were not "God conscious," they were obediently going to Shiloh, as the law commanded, to do service for and worship the Lord. As we find our place in God by continuously seeking Him with a pure heart, worshipping Him for who He is and what He has done, rather than expecting "things;" we will then be at the place where we will ask and it shall be given to us (Matthew 7:7). This was the case with Hannah. During one of the trips to Shiloh, she was very discouraged and sad, and was found praying outside of the temple, where Eli, the high priest, could hear. When Eli approached, he misunderstood her praying, believing that she was drunk, since her lips were moving and no sound was coming from them. After she replied to Eli's inquiry whether or not she was drunk, she told him her sorrow. Eli exclaimed, "Cheer up. May the Lord God of Israel grant you your petition, whatever it is!"

Hannah had already promised the Lord that if she were given a son, she would give him back to Him. It is evident that she had a close relationship with the Lord. She even understood the Nazarite vow stated in Numbers 6:1, 2, since she states clearly, "His hair shall not be cut." It is also very interesting to note that not only did God keep His part, but also Hannah kept her part (Judges 13:5).

Psalm 34:15 says, "The eyes of the Lord are upon the righteous, and his ears are open unto their cry." Hannah never gave up. She never retaliated against Peninah. Even though her loving husband could offer little encouragement, and even though she was at first misunderstood by the high priest, she continued to pursue the Lord. Similarly, each of us may face times of "barrenness" in our lives when nothing good seems to manifest in our work, service, or relationships. It is difficult to pray in faith when we feel so ineffective, but our consistent, fervent prayer opens the door for God to work in our lives. James 5:16 says, "The effectual, fervent, prayer of a righteous man availeth much," or, the Amplified Bible states, "The earnest (heartfelt, continued) prayer of a righteous man makes tremendous power available [dynamic in its working]!"

One of the more interesting points of this story is that after Hannah heard the blessing from Eli concerning her prayer, she returned to her husband with joy. She was no longer melancholy, discouraged, or sad. In fact, she goes back to resume her normal life. She could now eat regularly, whereas, before she could not. What a display of faith! She was confident that God heard her prayer and she acted on that confidence that she had in God! This should be our reaction when we pray.

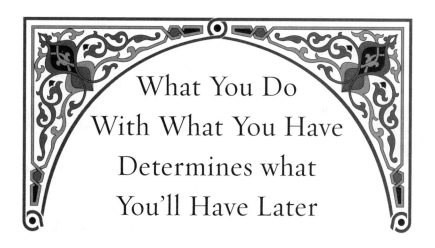

What You Do With What You Have Determines what You'll Have Later

RE: I Samuel 2

Because of her trust in God, Hannah conceived Samuel. Just after he was weaned, Hannah returned to Shiloh with her husband, Elkanah. The curse of barrenness now lifted, she could keep her vow to God by bringing her little son to the temple to begin his training. Hannah understands fully that she must follow through with her promise, and is glad to do so (I Samuel 1:11). She did not have a problem giving up what she wanted most, because she knew that her new son had come from God. The Bible teaches that our God will "withhold no good thing from those who walk uprightly," or, those who order their conduct right.

The modern church should feel the same way concerning our giving to God. We are only stewards, or managers, of everything we own. It is really not ours, but God has graciously distributed it to us. Yet, most of us complain about paying our tithe to the Lord. Why? Somehow we cannot justify that we are only the distributors for what God places in our hands. Meditate on this—He only asks us for ten percent, when He could ask us for ninety and give us ten! Because He loves us so much and wants to provide for our every need, He only desires for us to prove Him in this thing. He tells us that when we give to Him, He blesses that seed by giving back to us "good measure, pressed down, shaken together and running over" (Luke 6:38).

Hannah did what she did because she knew Samuel was a gift from heaven. When she presented him to Eli she was actually giving herself to the Lord. She was dedicating her entire future to God. Hannah was not really giving him up, but was rather returning him to God. We should ask ourselves the question, "Are we presenting tokens to God, or are we giving Him gifts of sacrifice?"

It should be noted that because of Hannah's honesty, in keeping her commitment to God, He gave her three more sons and two daughters (I Samuel 2:21). Again, this illustrates to us that God is faithful to His Word. We never hear of Peninah or her children again. God will bless us in ways we do not even expect, and all we must do is trust Him and follow His simple instruction! Sometimes God's blessings may not come immediately, but we must remember, as His Word declares, "A faithful man shall abound with blessings."

Train Up a Child

RE: I Samuel 2

The repeated condition of backsliding was apparent in Israel. To see how degenerated this great nation of God's people had become is really sorrowful. God's timing is perfect. It was no accident that God was miraculously preparing Samuel to fit into His plan. Let's look at the condition existing in the high priest's family at this time.

Eli, the high priest, had two sons—Hophni and Phineas. They were both priests by birthright; however, for God, this was not enough. I Samuel 2:12 explains that the sons of Eli were wicked men who did not love the Lord. Hosea 4:9, in the Living Bible, describes the situation, saying, "Like priests, like people." If the priests were wicked, the people were too. How sad to see these sons of Eli using the office of the priest for their own advantage. They displayed a lust for power, possessions; and control by taking advantage of their unearned position. Their contempt and arrogance toward the people and the worship of God endangered the integrity of the whole priesthood. They were taking parts of the sacrifices before they were offered to God on the altar and eating meat before the fat was burned off. This was in direct opposition and violation of God's law in Leviticus 3:3–5. In effect, they were treating God's offering with contempt. Offerings were given to show honor and respect to God while seeking forgiveness of sins, but Eli's sons were actually stealing them! To add to their sin, they were also laying with young women in the tabernacle (I Samuel 2:22). What a disgrace!

Perhaps one of the saddest parts of the story is the fact that Eli did very little to correct his sons. According to Numbers 15:22–31, Eli should have executed his sons. Out of his love for his own flesh and blood, it is no wonder why Eli chose not to confront the situation, but by giving in to their selfish actions, Eli let his sons ruin their lives, his life, and the lives of many others. Serious problems must be confronted, even if the consequences might be painful! Eli was guilty of honoring his sons above God by letting them continue in their sin in His most holy place.

Like Eli's sons, some people today treat the faith that others have in God with contempt. God harshly judges those who lead others astray and scorn their faith (Numbers 18:22).

In the middle of all of this, we read, in I Samuel 3:1, that messages from the Lord were very rare in those days. It is no wonder!

It was during this time of national spiritual crisis that Samuel was brought to the temple to be trained. Disobedience and a lack of concern dominated the priesthood and the congregation of Israel. It should be noted that the reason it seemed there was no voice from God was that they probably couldn't hear it! God was speaking, but there was no one close enough to God to really listen. Eli's house had degenerated the priesthood. Remember the condition of the nation from Hosea 6:9; "Like priests, like people."

In the midst of this, Samuel, a young man dedicated to the Lord, has been ministering to Eli. He hears the voice of God in the middle of the night, not knowing at first who it is. He assumes that it is Eli calling him, so he responds, "Here am I," but Eli explains twice that he was not the one calling. The third time Samuel goes to Eli, believing he called, Eli realizes it is the voice of the Lord. Eli tells Samuel to lie down and if he is called again, to respond, "Yes Lord, I'm listening." God then reveals His plan to Samuel regarding Eli, his sons, and Israel's plight.

One would think that Eli, not Samuel, would hear God's audible voice. Eli was older and more experienced; and he held the proper position to hear the voice of the Lord. But God's choice of command is based on spiritual condition, not on the natural! In finding faithful channels, God may use unexpected people. We must be prepared for the Lord to work at any time, at any place, and through anyone He chooses.

Imagine that all of Israel knew about Eli and his sons, just as they became aware of the spiritual condition of Samuel! I Samuel 3:20 says, "From the northernmost part of the land, Dan, to the Southernmost part, Beersheba, all Israel knew that Samuel was going to be a prophet of the Lord." How sad to see that Eli's sons, Hophni and Phineas, were wicked, but Samuel, the son of two godly people, Hannah and Elkanah, could hear the voice of God, even at a young and tender age. Eli might have been too busy to train his sons and to correct them, but Hannah kept her word. God's blessings upon Samuel surely had something to do with the faith and integrity of his parents.

We must see our spiritual position in training our children. It is serious business! The best part is that God did not leave us the total responsibility. God gave us His Word to instruct us how to teach them. Some of our children are "Samuels" and "Davids" and we must heed the call to show them the paths of righteousness and let them be everything God has created them to be.

We have a blessed assurance when we obey the Lord and bring up our children in the fear (respect) and admonition of the Lord. The Bible says, "Train up a child in the way he should go: and when he is old, he will not depart from it" (Proverbs 22:6).

The Tragic Results
of Sin

RE: I Samuel 4

Eli had been warned twice about the sins of his sons. The first time an unnamed prophet warned him. The second time he was warned by Samuel, who at an early age had heard the voice of God telling him about what He was going to do in Eli's life. Eli had spent his entire life in service to God. He had the great responsibility to oversee all the worship in Israel. However, in pursuing this great mission, he neglected his responsibilities in his own home.

During this time, the Philistines, Israel's major enemy, were constantly pressing inland against the Israelites. Descendants of Noah's son Ham, the Philistines were warlike people who were well established in the southwest part of Canaan. Another war had erupted between the cities of Ebenezer and Aphek. The Philistines had defeated Israel and 4,000 casualties were the result. When the battle was over, the leaders discussed their strategy for further attack. In fact, they questioned God, wondering why He had not given them victory, and had allowed them to be smitten (I Samuel 4:3). Can you imagine blaming God for problems they had created themselves? Remember, "You cannot serve God and mammon" (Matthew 6:24). You can't have a divided heart, and then expect God to intervene when you need Him. That doesn't mean that God will not meet you, but at that point you are using His grace.

Their decision was to bring the ark of God's covenant out of Shiloh, believing that somehow it might be a "good luck charm" (I Samuel 4:3, 4). This was almost like idol worship. In fact, all of Israel shouted with a great shout because they had a vain confidence. God was not, is not, and never will be our God only for times of crises! The Israelites' failure to defeat the Philistines was their own fault. Now they were ready to fall into greater condemnation because of their gross misuse of the glory of God. Israel had turned away from God. They were living on the memories of God's blessings. Israel wrongly assumed that since God had given them victory in the past, He would do it again, even though they had strayed far from Him. Spiritual victory comes from a continual relationship with God.

The Israelites then brought the ark of the covenant out of Shiloh. As the people carrying the ark came into the camp, there was great shouting. Eli's sons, Hophni and Phineas, were the two who carried the ark into battle. Imagine people living in sin, knowing their error, and still trying to use God's glory to save their necks! The Scripture says concerning prayer, "If I regard iniquity in my heart, the Lord will not hear me" (Psalm 66:18). The Philistines heard about the ark and were frightened by their recollection of stories of how God intervened for the Israelites when they left Egypt. Israel had turned away from God and now only clung to a form of godliness.

Perhaps one of the more interesting verses in the Bible appears in I Samuel 4:9. In the Philistine camp we can hear these words spoken out— "Quit yourselves like men, and fight." In other words: Act like the men you are! Conduct yourself like a man! Sometimes the world acts more like it should than the church does. They had established, in their minds, that they were not going to be slaves to the Hebrews, as the Hebrews had been slaves to them.

Notice the text in I Samuel 4:10 in the Living Bible, "So the Philistines fought desperately and Israel was defeated again." Thirty thousand (30,000) men were killed that day and the prophecy of I Samuel 2:34 came to pass. Hophni and Phineas were killed the same day. Then, after hearing news from the battlefield that the ark was taken and thousands of soldiers were dead, including his sons, Eli, 98 years old, fell backward and died. The widow of Phineas went into labor after hearing the news, and just before dying, she asked that the child be named "Ichabod," meaning, "the glory has departed."

Eli was Israel's judge and high priest. His death marked the end of the dark period of the judges when most of the nation ignored God. Although Samson was also a judge, his career saw the transition from Israel's rule by judges to the nation's monarchy. After forty years of horror under Eli's reign, the nation wondered if Samuel would be a vessel of God used to bring revival for Israel's next century. They were in dire need of it!

A Requiem For Eli

RE: I Samuel 5, 6

There are many lessons to be learned from Eli's life. The recognition and respect he had earned in his public life was a result of how he handled his private life. He may have been an excellent priest, but he was a poor parent. By this failure, he opened the door for his sons to bring him grief and ruin. He lacked three important qualities for effective parenting:

1. Parental discipline
2. Firm resolve
3. Corrective action

Eli responded to situations by "band-aiding" them rather than curing them, therefore, never resolving them. Even his responses tended to be weak. When God pointed out the errors of Hophni and Phineas, by an unnamed prophet, Eli did little to correct them. As God spoke to little Samuel, telling him what He was going to do, Eli simply responded, "Let him do what he thinks is best" (I Samuel 3:18).

The difference between what Eli did and what a good parent would do is simple. God gave warning, spelled out the consequences of disobedience, and then acted. Eli only warned. Children need to learn that their parents' words and actions go together. Both love and discipline must be spoken as well as followed through and acted out.

Eli had another problem. During his many years spent as high priest, Eli became more concerned with the symbols of his religion than with the God they represented. For Eli, the ark of the covenant had become a relic to be protected, rather than a reminder of the Protector. Like many people, Eli's faith shifted from the Creator to the created. Tangible things have no power in themselves. Buildings, temples, etc., are only a representation of God. They possess no power without the people. In the same connotation, the Bible must not be used as a sacred relic. It is a book that contains the words of God, but is ineffective without the Author of it, alive on the inside of the reader.

Hebrews 6:12 explains that we must follow after those who, "through faith and patience inherit the promises." The first part of the verse states, "That ye be not slothful." We cannot slack on any of the responsibilities we have from God. There is no way we will ever grow to full stature in Christ unless we become both hearers and doers of the Word of God.

Israelite's blessing— Philistine's Curse

RE: I Samuel 5

Sometimes the world seems to know more about the blessings of God than believers. The Philistines had realized that the ark of the covenant, God's presence among the Jews, had brought victory to them. They decided that if they could get the ark, the following would be part of the result:

1. Israel would no longer have supernatural help.
2. The Philistines would now have supernatural help themselves.

The Philistines were in for a very big surprise!

The Philistines were "polytheistic." They worshipped many gods. The more "gods" they had to worship, the more secure they felt. Dagon was one of their gods, set up in their major city of Ashod. The Philistines believed that he was the god who sent rain and assured a bountiful harvest. Possibly, one reason the Philistines wanted the ark was to add to their "security" list of gods. Probably more prominent in their thinking was their remembering what they had seen. The Philistines knew of the great results Israel had with the ark. From the Scripture, we can probably assume, based on the disrespect the leadership outwardly displayed for the ark of the covenant, that the nation of Israel did not fully realize that this ark was the glory of God. Also, they probably could not recognize what God had already done with it.

In chapter 5, we see that the Philistines took the ark and set it up near Dagon in Ashdod. The next morning they found Dagon on its face. The people fixed the statue and again, the following morning, they found it on the ground with its head and hands cut off. The Bible clearly states it was "on the ground before the ark of the Lord." On top of that, they were afflicted with painful tumors (KJV calls them "emerods") and were plagued with rats. This threw them into panic. There were five major cities among the Philistines and the ark was sent to three of them in an attempt to resolve the situation. In each alternative city, something similar happened (I Samuel 5:9). The plague was so bad that many were dying. The judgment of God had come.

The Philistines thought they had defeated God because they had beaten Israel and captured the ark. They soon learned that no one defeats God. Their "sweet victory" turned sour as God began to pass judgment on them. What was victory and success for Israel was defeat, failure, and destruction for the Philistines. How pitiful to think that Israel had fallen so low. They allowed the very presence of God to be taken from them, causing them sad defeat. The Bible says in Galatians 6:7, 8, "Be not deceived; God is not mocked for whatsoever a man soweth, that shall he also reap. For he that soweth to his flesh shall of the flesh reap corruption; but he that soweth to the Spirit shall of the Spirit reap life everlasting."

We must choose between Spiritual decay (death) and everlasting life. Let us guard what God has given us, learn not to take Him for granted, and lock the door on the Devil.

The Return of the Ark—Return to Worship

RE: I Samuel 6, 7

Because it had brought devastation and destruction to them everywhere it had gone, the Philistines chose to get rid of the ark. They decided to test the ark by hitching cows with newborn calves to a cart with the ark on it. "By doing so," they said, "we will see if the cows go to wherever they want." Normally, a cow that has just had a newborn calf will immediately return to its baby. But, as the cows began to walk, they went directly back to Bethshemesh, where the Israelites were. Once again, by the mercy of God, the glory had returned.

The men of Bethshemesh sacrificed a burnt offering to God (I Samuel 6:15). Wherever there is a burnt offering in the Old Testament, it is representative of renewing a relationship with God. They were worshipping God by rededicating their lives to Him and demonstrating their willingness to start over. Notice the outright display of their disobedience. Although they had been warned of what they could and could not do (Numbers 4:20), there were many who, in direct opposition, looked upon the ark and were killed. Because of their disobedience, God carried out His promised judgment. Their worship of God was not acceptable, and this teaches us a valuable lesson.

Worship extols God for who He is, in contrast to praise, which eulogizes God for what He has done. If this is true, then worship is always limited to our knowledge of God, for we cannot extol God beyond our concept of Him. There can be no strange fire on the altar. God is seeking worshippers who know more about the person of God than the principles of God. Many give to God, receive from God, and work on His behalf, but they never enter into an intimate relationship with Him. This is far beneath God's desires and plans for His children. He wants us to know Him, not only to know of Him.

To illustrate further their shallow knowledge of God and total disregard for His clear instruction, the Israelites sent a message to Kirjathjearim, asking them to come and take the ark. The Israelites no longer wanted the ark to stay with them in Bethshemesh. They did not understand the God they were serving. If they would have learned of Him and followed His plan, they would have been able to understand His heart and avoid this terrible fate.

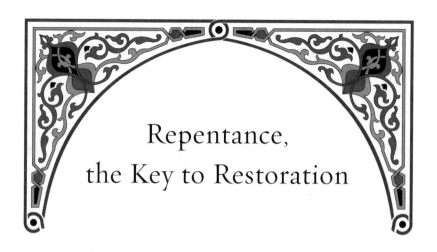

Repentance,
the Key to Restoration

RE: I Samuel 7

After supernatural transportation (the cows), the ark of the covenant had arrived at Bethshemesh. But again, in total disobedience and disrespect to the Lord, the men of the city looked upon the ark and the result was seventy casualties. A cry went out to the people of Kirjathjearim to take away the ark. Can you imagine that for these many years the ark (glory of God) had been missing, and now it is returned by two cows! Then, because of the tragedy of their own disobedience, the Jews wanted the ark out of their city. Instead of repenting right there and turning back to God, as little children, they began to complain.

The men from Kirjathjearim came, took the ark, and brought it to the hillside home of Abinadab. There, they gave it to Abinadab's son, Eleazar, to keep. The ark would remain there twenty years, during which time Israel would mourn sorrowfully because it seemed the Lord had abandoned them. In reality, by allowing the ark to be moved, they abandoned God. The ark had been put away, like an unwanted picture in an attic. How easy it is to complain about our problems, even to God, while we refuse to change and do what He requires. We want to blame God, rather than accept the responsibility for our failures. We can never receive God's guidance in our lives until we acknowledge our own failure.

Notice Samuel's words from I Samuel 7:3; he says, "If ye do return unto the Lord with all your hearts, then put away the strange gods and Ashtaroth from among you, and prepare your hearts unto the Lord, and serve Him only: and He will deliver you out of the hand of the Philistines." The key to victory was a total turning to God. How could they have peace with God while they had idols in their houses? How could they have the joy of the Lord with sin in their lives? The key verse is in I Samuel 7:4, which says, "Then the children of Israel did put away Baalim and Ashtaroth, and served the Lord only." This was a true sign of repentance for their sins.

Samuel then instructed the repentant Israelites to go to Mizpeh, where he would pray for them. When the Philistines heard of this great crowd at Mizpah, they attacked, and Israel was frightened. They asked Samuel to pray. He set a sacrifice before the Lord, and while he was preparing it, God sent a mighty thunder on the Philistines from heaven. They were thrown into confusion and smitten before the Israelites (I Samuel 7:9, 10). God is faithful!

The Secrets
of Remembering

RE: I Samuel 7:9

Revelation 2:5 tells us the Ephesian church was told to "remember where they had fallen from." They were told to repent and return to doing their first works. If not, the Holy Spirit said He would remove their candlestick. The "candlestick" was symbolic of the seven-branched candlestick in the temple used to give light.

David said in Psalm 20:7, "Some trust in chariots, and some in horses but we will remember the name of the Lord our God." David was really speaking of empires, kingdoms, and great armies that had, at one time, risen to power, but eventually became as dust. David knew that the true might of the nation was not in weaponry, but in worship. It was not in "firepower," but in God's power! That's why all was worth remembering God!

When Israel decided to remember God, even after all the terrible years of apostasy during the judges, God came on the scene to help them. In Psalm 46:1, we read, "God is our refuge, and our strength, a very present help in trouble." The Bible also tells us, "The eyes of the Lord run to and fro looking to show Himself strong on behalf of those whose heart is perfect [or upright] towards him." God wants us to remember Him and honor Him.

After God supernaturally responded to Israel's cry for help through the prophet of God, Samuel took a stone and set it up between Mizpah and Shen and called the name of it "Ebenezer," or, "this stone of help." It was to be a memorial of God's help in the midst of great trouble. While we must be careful that memorials do not become idols, they can help us to remember God's victories, and they can help us gain confidence and strength for the present.

The Bible goes on to explain, in I Samuel 7:13, that after this great Israeli victory, the Philistines "came no more unto the coasts of Israel because the hand of the Lord was against them all the days of Samuel." The "days of Samuel" were approximately one hundred years.

The Blessing
of Remembering

RE: Deuteronomy 6-8

The key verse to consider, before discussing the chapter before us, is found in Deuteronomy 5:29 in the Living Bible, and says, "O that they would always have such a heart for Me, wanting to obey My commandments. Then all will go well with them in the future, and with their children throughout all generations!"

As we approach the truth of the blessing of remembering, we must consider the background. Approximately forty years earlier, the Israelites could have enjoyed the blessings of Canaan if they would have been quick to obey. They knew the land "flowed with milk and honey," since all twelve spies brought back the same report. However, ten spies and most of the people were possessed with a "grasshopper" complex. They were dominated by fear and failure. Through Moses, God was preparing them for what they were going to face. God was determined, through the hands of Moses, to help His people avoid the same mistake they had made before. He did this by whetting their appetite with the blessing ahead of them, and then clearly describing the conditions to be met.

The oft-repeated words, "If you obey," dominate much of the book of Deuteronomy, as God sets the standard for blessing: obedience. But, there is another dominating phrase, "Don't forget." The Lord reminded Israel of all the things He did for them in the past. In Deuteronomy 8:14,

He reminds them of their deliverance out of bondage in Egypt, and in Deuteronomy 8:15, 16, He reminds them of the miracles in the wilderness; their protection from serpents and scorpions, the water from the rock, and the fresh manna for food. He begins by saying, "Beware that in your plenty you don't forget the Lord your God and begin to disobey Him."

The Lord had promised them prosperity and blessing. He said, "When you come unto the land, there will be cities of good things. These will be wells you didn't dig, cities you didn't build, vineyards and olive trees you didn't plant, and you will eat until you are full." The Lord promised them that they would drive out nations before them and that He would deliver kings into their hands. He declared that no one would be able to stand against them. He promised full prosperity, fine homes to live in, large herds and flocks, and multiplied silver and gold. He then added that it was important for them to be sure they would not become proud and forget where they had come from (Deuteronomy 7:16–24; 8:11–14). All of this was promised just for remembering!

Some say God's word of blessing and prosperity could not be taken for all Christians, especially if taken from Old Testament history. They also try to explain that Old Testament prophecy was only relative to certain times and places, and it no longer is true in the church dispensation. A simple reading of Galatians 3:14 should settle that issue forever; it says, "That the blessings of Abraham might come on the Gentiles." Verse 29 of the same chapter in Galatians tells us, "And if ye be Christ's, then are ye Abraham's seed, and heirs according to the promise."

All of God's blessings come wrapped in responsibility. However, none of God's blessings are "automatic" or "unconditional." The Lord instructed very clearly that His people were to train their children "in the way they should go," or, "by the Word of God." They were instructed to teach them to talk about the Word at all times! He promised that if they would do so, they would get into the land He promised, because He was giving it to them. He instructed them not to forget that all the credit belonged to Him for taking them out of slavery in Egypt and bringing them into a blessed land.

To put it even more simply—to forget would be the exact opposite of remembering. God specifically told them, do not forget where you came from and who got you where you are. After explaining that, He confirmed that if they continued to obey Him, remembered who He was and what He had done, and did all that He commanded, all would go well for them, and they would be able to go in and possess the good land that the Lord promised their ancestors. He even told them that they would overthrow all the enemies living in the land as He had previously promised (Deuteronomy 6:18, 19).

God then gave them the "flip side." If they forgot about Him, and worshipped other gods, He declared that they would "certainly perish." Just as the Lord caused other nations in the past to perish, that would be their fate, too, if they did not obey the Lord their God (Deuteronomy 8:19, 20).

If this is the condition God will bless us on, it is well worth it to remember rather than to pay the price of forgetting.

The Reward of Training a Child

RE: Deuteronomy 11

While we are discussing child training in this lesson, it should be recognized that it is not a truth exclusively reserved for children, but can aptly apply to adults as well.

Proverbs 22:15 says, "Foolishness is bound in the heart of a child, but the rod of correction shall drive it far from him." The Amplified Bible translates the word "correction" as "discipline." We also read in Hebrews 12:9 that we had "fathers of our flesh" that disciplined us. This is a statement that verifies the fact that it is the responsibility of parents to correct and discipline their children. While from a physical standpoint, in the natural, there is great reward in an unspoiled child, there is greater reward, and greater responsibility, to do something beyond the physical, in the spiritual realm.

In the same chapter in Proverbs, verse 6, Solomon makes an incredible statement, saying, "Train up a child in the way he should go, and when he is old he will not depart from it." The Living Bible calls the way he should go "the right path." This was exactly what God was telling Israel concerning their children as they were preparing to enter the Promised Land. Although parents rarely ever admit it, our children become duplicates of what we are. This was the reason the Lord told the parents first to be doers of the Word by keeping the commandments before them day and night to observe and to do them. (Deuteronomy 11:18). He proceeded to say these important words to them in Deuteronomy 11:19–21 (Living Bible), "Teach them to your children. Talk about them when you are sitting at home, when you are out walking, at bedtime, and before breakfast! Write them upon the doors of your houses and upon your gates, so that as long as there is sky above the earth, you and your children will enjoy the good life awaiting you in the land the Lord has promised you."

The message is very clear. God says by training our children in His Word, being an example of it, and constantly reminding them of it, it will produce great results. It is true today just as it was then. The Israelites would enjoy the blessings of their new land forever by simply teaching their children to love God with all their hearts, as they were supposed to.

The Responsibility of Training a Child

RE: Numbers 14:31—33

It is so sad to think back to when Israel finally got back to the place at the Jordan after some forty years of wandering in the wilderness and see what really took place to prepare them for the entry. God told them He would cut off all those people who were doubters and murmurers from going into the Promised Land (I Corinthians 10:5). He then said He would allow their children to go into the land. He had a very good reason for this. The children had not been spoiled yet, and the opportunity for them to grow up and be trained was still possible. No wonder Moses insisted in Deuteronomy (which is really the book of the summary of Moses' training sessions with Israel) that they teach their children the Word. That principle has never changed. God is still in the New Testament, teaching us the same principles. Let us examine it further and review some interesting examples.

In II Timothy 1:5, we find that Paul wrote to Timothy reminding him of the faith that was deposited in him through his grandmother, Lois, and his mother, Eunice. He was obviously very influenced by their godly lives. We have further proof of this in his writing to Timothy in II Timothy 3:14, 15, when he says to continue in the things that he has learned as a child. He goes on to show that the Holy Scriptures were the things he learned as a child. It is so interesting to see how much influence this family had on Timothy's call to the ministry. Proverbs says, "Through wisdom a house is built." The Bible describes wisdom as nothing more than the Word of God. Romans 10:17 also says, "Faith cometh by hearing and hearing by the Word of God." This should be evidence enough to prove that there will be great reward in training up our children by the Word of God. In II Timothy 3:15, the phrase, "And that from a child thou hast known the Holy Scriptures," proves Lois and Eunice taught Timothy the truth of God's Word. It is also notable that Paul tells Timothy to keep it up by "studying to show himself approved unto God!" We must follow the example of those who, through faith and patience, inherit the promises.

Sometimes We Really Get What We Ask For

RE: I Samuel 8

It was not until the end of Samuel's long tenure as judge over Israel that he appointed his two eldest sons, Joel and Abijah, to judge in his place. Unfortunately, they were greedy for money, accepted bribes, and were corrupt in the administration of justice. It is a real pity that a godly man like Samuel had such ungodly sons. It appears that when they got to office, the power went to their heads. We have no indication from Scripture that Samuel was at fault with his training of his children, as we did with Eli and his sons. Apparently, they decided to turn from godly counsel and do their own thing, although we are not sure of the exact case.

The people were terribly upset at their leadership and asked Samuel to "give them a king like all the other nations" (I Samuel 8:5, 6). Here were their reasons:

1. Samuel's sons were not fit to lead Israel.
2. The twelve tribes of Israel continually had problems working to-gether because each tribe had its own leader and territory. They hoped a king would unite them into one.
3. They wanted, once again, to be like the neighboring nations.

This is the very thing that God did not want. Having a king would make it easy to forget who their real leader was. God was disappointed because, once again, the people were rejecting Him as their leader. The Israelites wanted laws, an army, and a human monarch in the place of God. They were seeking a human solution to goals that were beyond their ability to achieve.

In I Samuel 8:6, from the Living Bible, the people requested a king to judge them. Samuel prayed, because he knew this was not what God wanted. "Do as they say," the Lord replied in verses 7–9, "for I am the one they are rejecting, not you. They don't want me to be their King any longer. Just as they have done before, they are forsaking me, and serving other gods. But, warn them about what it will be like to have a king." As instructed, Samuel told the people that if they wanted their own way they could have it, but they would pay a great price for their decision.

Samuel tried to persuade them to do good by explaining all the reasons it would be a burden to have a king. He concluded by telling them, "You will shed bitter tears because of this king you are demanding, but the Lord will not help you." Still the people refused to listen to Samuel's warning. This very decision would bring serious spiritual charges against Israel for generations to come (I Samuel 8:11–19).

It is better to follow God's advice, His path, and His ways to get His blessing in our lives, than to settle for the destruction "second best" will bring (See Proverbs 3:5, 6).

Divine Guidance
of the First King

RE: I Samuel 9, 10

Oftentimes, God moves by what appears to be the strangest of circumstances. This next story surely is one of those times. While we know that certain things that happen in life may be very distressing and troublesome at the time they happen, we also know, according to Romans 8:28, "All things work together for good to them that love God and who are the called according to His purpose." The story of Israel's first king, Saul, is one of these kinds of stories.

As I Samuel 9 opens, we already know from the previous chapter that Jehovah is going to honor Israel's request for a king. In this narrative of I Samuel 9, amazing events unfold around the life of Saul, the son of Kish, a rich influential man (I Samuel 9:1, Living Bible). We also know that Saul was the most handsome man in Israel. Scripture describes him as having stood "head and shoulders" above anyone else in the land. His father sent him out on a mission to find his lost donkeys that had strayed. Although it is probably hard for us to believe, in those days, donkeys were all-purpose animals. They were like the pick-up-trucks of Bible times. They were used for transportation, hauling, and farming, and they were considered a necessity. Even the poorest family owned at least one. To own many donkeys was a sign of wealth, and to lose them was a disaster. The many donkeys Saul's father owned were a sure sign of his wealth.

After searching for the lost donkeys through all of the hill country of Benjamin, and much of the surrounding area, Saul and his servant were about ready to give up and go home. They thought that perhaps Kish, his father, would be worried about him. Beginning to journey back home, Saul's servant had an idea. He told Saul that there was a prophet that lived in the city where they were, and that all the people held him in high honor because everything he said came true. He suggested that they find him and perhaps he would be able to tell them where the donkeys were (I Samuel 9:6).

About the same time Saul's servant had the "idea" to find the prophet concerning Saul's donkey, the Lord spoke to Samuel and told him that he was sending a young man from Benjamin for him to anoint as the leader of the nation. When Saul met Samuel, and he told him what God wanted him to do, Saul tried to talk himself out of it, explaining that he was "from the smallest tribe in Israel," and that his family was "the least important of all the families of the tribe." Samuel then explained that the donkeys Saul was looking for had been found, and as they feasted, and Saul heard more, he realized that he must accept his responsibility, and as he did, he prepared himself to be crowned king.

Often we think that things "just happen" to us, but as we learn from this story about Saul, God often uses common occurrences to lead us where He wants. It is important to evaluate all situations and recognize what is a divine appointment designed by God to shape our lives. Although it is always supernatural direction when we are living for Him, some of the circumstances may be very "natural." What we may consider bad situations may be the greatest things God uses to direct our paths.

The Anointing of the First King

RE: I Samuel 10

When an Israelite king took office, he was not only crowned, he was anointed. The coronation was the political act of establishing the king as ruler. The anointing was the religious act of making the king God's representative to the people. A priest or a prophet always anointed a king. The oil was poured over the king's head to symbolize the presence and power of the Holy Spirit in his life. The anointing ceremony was to remind the king of his great responsibility to lead the people by God's wisdom and not his own.

Samuel the prophet was setting Saul up to be anointed as the new king of Israel. He gave him instructions of where to go and what would happen when he got there. In his instructions, he told him that when he got to the Grove of Tabor, he would meet three men on their way to Bethel, who would give him two loaves of bread. He was then to go to Gibeah, which was the Hill of God, probably to reside there. It is believed by some that this was a high place where God was worshipped.

"There," Samuel said, "you will meet a band of prophets who will be playing various instruments and prophesying as they come, and the Spirit of the Lord shall come upon you, and you too will prophesy and you will be turned into another man."

We can see from this that the Holy Spirit is who makes the difference in our lives. Samuel was very specific in telling Saul about the supernatural anointing coming upon him. It was more than ceremony and it was more than circumstance. It was the presence of the Holy Spirit and the divine will of God. It is the divine enabling of the Holy Spirit that makes the difference in our lives. The Holy Spirit is our comforter and teacher (John 14:26). He encourages us and instructs us, and He is our anointing to know. He abides in us to make up for any human lack that we may possess (I John 2:20, 27).

Notice what the Scripture says of Saul in I Samuel 10:6. It says he "turned into another man," or, more literally, he had a different attitude. This is exactly what the Holy Spirit will do in the life of a person when a decision is made to make Jesus their Lord. Thank God for the Holy Spirit, who can make the difference in our lives! Like Saul, always remember, even though you may start out right, it is important to maintain your walk with God! With such a supernatural beginning, it is sad to watch such a chosen vessel lose the anointing through pride and disobedience. It is not how we start that counts; it is how we finish.

Disobedience, the Seed of Destruction

RE: I Samuel 12—15

Soon after Saul had been anointed to be king, and after the Spirit of God came upon him, he returned to his hometown of Gibeah. Upon his arrival, he was told about the Ammonites, a marauding tribe from the east of Jordan who had come to try to disgrace Israel. They wanted to gouge out the right eye of each of the people of Jabesh-Gilead and make them servants. When the news got back to Gibeah, everyone began to cry. Eventually, the news got to Saul, while he was plowing in the field. I Samuel 11:6 says, "The Spirit of the Lord came strongly upon him and he became angry." Led by the Spirit of God, he mobilized his troops and set out to rescue his people at Jabesh-Gilead. There, he slaughtered the Ammonites.

How interesting it is to note that many times we use the gifts that God has graced and blessed us with to gloat in our own accomplishments. Saul's military power was not because he had graduated from some training academy, but because the anointing of the Holy Spirit was upon him. Many times, especially in ministry, we look to the person, and glorify them, rather than glorifying God in them. This is the reason why Samuel decided to give the people a strong message. After reminding them of where God had brought them from, and how He had blessed them, he gave them a solemn warning directing his comments specifically at the newly chosen king. Saul, in I Samuel 12:14, 15, said, "Now if you will fear and worship the Lord, and listen to His commandments and not rebel against the Lord, and if both you and your king follow the Lord your God, then all will be well. But, if you rebel against the Lord's commandments and refuse to listen to Him, then his hand will be as heavy upon you as it was upon your ancestors."

The warning had been given over and over again—don't turn from the Lord. Actually, what Samuel was saying of the Lord was the same as John 15:6 tells us, "Without me you can do nothing." Our help and our strength are not in our ability, but rather in our availability to God. Samuel said in I Samuel 12:24, "Trust the Lord and sincerely worship Him; think of all the tremendous things he has done for you." But if you continue to sin, you and your king will be destroyed." This was truly a solemn warning to all of us. Let us keep our eyes on Jesus, the Author and Finisher of our faith (Hebrews 12:2).

While God had granted the nation a king, His commandments and requirements for their lives had not changed. God was still to be their true king, and both Saul and the people were to be subject to His law. No person is ever exempt from God's law. No human involvement is ever outside of His jurisdiction. God is the true King of every area of life. We must recognize His kingship and submit to Him in obedience (1 Samuel 13).

After only one year as king, Saul was already on the brink of forgetting this important principle. He was ready to forget what Samuel had warned him about. As chapter 13 opens, Saul has selected 3,000 special troops and begins to attack the garrison of the Philistines at Gibeah. Jonathan, his son, is in command of 1,000 of these special troops. Jonathan's leadership was very successful and his troops literally destroyed the Philistines at Gibeah.

The news traveled fast throughout the Philistine camp and they began to recruit a mighty army of 3,000 chariots, 6,000 horsemen, and so many troops that they were "as thick as sand along the seashore." When all of Israel heard of this, they lost their nerve entirely and began to run away and hide in caves, behind rocks, in thickets, and in whatever other shelter they could find. In verse 8, we find the people were truly in fear. Samuel had told Saul to wait seven days for his arrival, but when he still didn't come and Saul's troops were rapidly slipping away, he decided to sacrifice the burnt offerings and the peace offerings himself. Saul's impatience caused him to act against God's will.

Thinking that the ritual of the sacrifice alone was enough to help, he confused the act of sacrifice with the God of the sacrifice.

Impatience can drive us to make foolish and rash decisions that disagree with the Word of God. Numbers 18:5 (Living Bible) says, "Remember only the priests are to perform the sacred duties within the sanctuary and the altar. If you follow these instructions the wrath of God will never fall upon any of the people of Israel for violating this law." When Samuel finally arrived, he exclaimed, "You fool, you have disobeyed the commandment of the Lord your God. He was planning to make your descendants kings of Israel forever. Now your dynasty must end, for the Lord wants a man who will obey him."

Saul had many excuses for his disobedience. He told Samuel, "My men were scattering from me, and you hadn't arrived yet as you said you would, and the Philistines were at Michmash, ready for battle." (I Samuel 13:10–12)

We act like Saul many times, often trying to gloss over our mistakes and sins, trying to justify and "spiritualize" our actions because of our "special" circumstances. Our excuses are nothing more than disobedience. God knows our true motives. Our excuses only satisfy us as we offer them. God forgives, restores, and blesses only when we are honest about our sin. By trying to hide his sins behind excuses, Saul lost his kingship. Samuel says, "And now He [the Lord] has discovered the man He wants and has already appointed him as king over His people, for you have not obeyed the Lord's commandment" (I Samuel 13:14).

Saul had a stubborn spirit, and this is further exemplified in I Samuel 15. Once again, he disobeyed the commandment of the Lord, which was to destroy everything in battle against the Amalekites. He kept the best of the sheep and oxen and the fattest of the lambs. In fact, he kept everything that appealed to him (I Samuel 15:9). Again, through Samuel, the Lord spoke to Saul and told him how he had again dishonored the Lord. The seeds of destruction had been sown by his total disobedience to the Lord. Then, the seeds were watered and fed when he blamed others and made excuses for his failure. A famous and often quoted verse is spoken by Samuel in I Samuel 15:22, as he says, "To obey is better than sacrifice." Nothing we do will make up for disobedience. God cannot be conned.

First impressions of Saul were deceiving. His handsome outward appearance contradicted the tendencies of his personality that, far too often, were contrary to the Word of God. He was God's chosen leader; but God's choice did not imply that Saul was capable of being king on his own. Saul could only be successful as he obeyed God. Our skills and talents make us tools, but our failures and shortcomings remind us; we need God! Without Him we can do nothing, but with Him we can do all things, as He continually strengthens us (Proverbs 3:5, 6; Phil. 4:13)!

Words, the Controlling Force of Life

RE: I Samuel 14

KEY TEXT: "Death and life are in the power of the tongue: and they that love it shall eat the fruit thereof" (Proverbs 18:21).

Saul found that after Samuel had left him at Gilgal, only 600 soldiers remained with him, and his disobedience had cut him off and removed him from being king. Returning to Gibeah, in the land of Benjamin, they found themselves at a virtual standoff with the Philistines. In fact, the Philistines had divided up into three different groups and surrounded them. One of the saddest verses you will ever read throughout the Old Testament history of Israel is I Samuel 13:19, which says, "Now there was no smith [blacksmith] found throughout all the land of Israel: for the Philistines said, lest the Hebrews make them swords or spears." The next verse shows how low we become at times in our lives when we take our eyes off of our only source, God; "But all Israel went down to the Philistines to sharpen his share [sickle], and his coulter [plow tool], and his ax, and his mattock [hoe] so that in the day of battle there was no sword or spear found in the hand of any of the people except Saul and Saul's son Jonathan" (I Samuel 13:20–22). Imagine this! The Philistines had full control over Israel's weapons to put them at a disadvantage and made them vulnerable to defeat. Only God's divine help could get them out of this mess that they again had gotten themselves into.

In the middle of this situation, Jonathan and his armourbearer (literally his bodyguard) had secretly disappeared to go out to reach the Philistine garrison (I Samuel 14:6). Jonathan said to his armourbearer, "Let's go across to those heathens." Now, notice these words; "Perhaps the Lord will do a miracle for us. For it makes no difference to Him how many enemy troops there are." The KJV says, "For there is no restraint to the Lord to save by many or by few." Jonathan had used his words to voice what he believed. Literally, by his words, by his confession, he set the stage for God's miracle deliverance. As they approached the Philistine camp, they were spotted, and the Philistines cried out to them in I Samuel 14:12, "Come up to us, we will shew you a thing." This was their signal to attack.

Listen again to the words that come out of Jonathan's mouth to his armourbearer—"Come up after me: for the Lord hath delivered them into the hand of Israel." Jonathan and his bodyguard were not much of a force to attack the huge Philistine army. BUT, while everyone else was afraid, they trusted God. They knew that the size of the enemy had no relationship to God's ability to help them. God honors the faith of those who trust Him and believe His Word.

There is a great truth about confessing your faith revealed in this story. Notice not only that Jonathan said something, but notice what he said; "The Lord hath delivered them into the hand of Israel." He made his statement past tense, while in fact, there had been no battle fought, no enemy conquered, and realistically, the odds were so overwhelming that it would almost seem like a ridiculous thing to say! It's amazing that when we read the Scripture, in hindsight we have such an easy time calling this faith; yet when someone today makes similar faith statements, they are highly criticized. If it can be true in the Old Testament then it is equally true today. We express fear or faith with our words. We release the ability of God by speaking God's Word.

God's Word in our mouths produces a force called faith in the human spirit. If it is abundant in your heart, get it into your mouth. Jesus said in Matthew 12:34, "Out of the abundance of the heart, the mouth speaketh." It starts a dynamic that generates a spiritual force that is unstoppable! Glory to God!

In John 8:26, Jesus said that He spoke only that which He heard His father say. If we will do the same, we will begin to see situations change in our lives that may seem as hopeless as Jonathan's. We should begin to say, "I have the wisdom of God. I have the direction of God. I have the faith of God. I hear the voice of the Good Shepherd, and whatsoever things I desire when I pray, according to the will of God, I know that He hears, and I know that I have the petition that I desire of Him!" Do not pray the problem—pray the answer!

Jonathan declared his victory. The power of life and victory were in his heart and expressed with his tongue. The victory did not come in the battle; it came before the battle. God ordains success for us. We must accept it, speak it, and live it. Jonathan pursued the Philistines and killed about twenty of them, leaving their dead bodies over a large piece of ground and causing panic among them. God also caused a great earthquake to increase their fear, and they turned on each other and killed themselves. One man's faith-filled words brought victory to an army. We will have the same results if we do the same thing—believe God. If God is for us, who will dare to stand against us? (1 Samuel 14:15, 20)

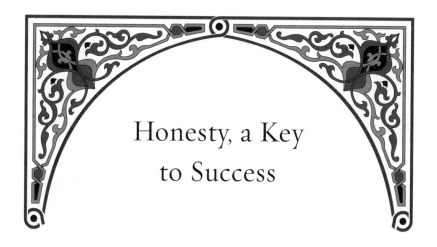

Honesty, a Key to Success

RE: I Samuel 14, 15

As Jonathan and his servant were declaring their victory, out in the battlefield, against the Philistines, Saul was listening to the Philistine cry of hysteria and confusion getting louder and louder. With his 600 men, he rushed out into the battlefield and found the enemy in terrible confusion, turning on each other and killing themselves (Samuel 14:20–23). God had given them supernatural victory over the alien army.

It is sad to see Saul did not learn any lesson from what happened. He remained impetuous, making vows he could not keep, and he still refused to wholeheartedly depend on the Lord (I Samuel 14:38, 39). He continued to shun his faults, transferring the blame to everyone else. He even went so far as to make a rash ruling declaring that whoever ate any food on the chosen day of the fast he ordered would be put to death. This vow was very foolish, because Jonathan, his own son, and other soldiers in battle, had no way of knowing they were to keep this vow. Unaware of this vow, Jonathan ate honey off of a stick on the chosen day. When confronted with this vow, the people declared that they would not allow this good young man to be put to death since he had trusted God and saved Israel. Saul was really more interested in protecting his image than enforcing his vow. We must learn to admit our mistakes and be more interested in being right in God's sight than in what is favorable to ourselves and pleasing to men.

Notable in this story is the fact that God never asked people to make vows, but when they did, He expected them to keep them. Saul had made a vow so impetuous that it risked his own son's life. Fortunately for Saul, the people intervened and spared Jonathan's life.

Jonathan's spiritual character was a striking contrast to Saul's. He admitted what he had done and did not try to make excuses. Although he was unaware of Saul's orders, he was willing to suffer the consequences of his actions. What an example to follow! Jonathan obviously had a heart after God. It was his boldness and courage that brought victory to Israel, and then he admits to a harmless act hastily deemed an executable offense by his father. Proverbs 28:13 in the Living Bible says, "A man who refuses to admit his mistakes can never be successful. But if he confesses and forsakes them, he gets another chance." Saul had really set himself up for destruction by his arrogance, rashness, and dishonesty. A reading of the Bible text will show the clear contrast between father and son, and will prove that honesty is the only policy in the kingdom of God.

Pride, a Key to Destruction

RE: I Samuel 15

Proverbs 1:24, 25 in the Living Bible says, "I have called you so often but still you won't come. I have pleaded, but all in vain. For you have spurned my counsel and reproof."

To hear wisdom's advice, we must be listening and willing to do what wisdom demands. We cannot let pride stand in the way. Pride is thinking more highly of our own wisdom than of God's. If we think we know better than God, we have fallen into foolish pride. When we feel we have no need of God's direction, we are ignoring the bridge that connects us to Him. That bridge is humility. Pride will lead us to do whatever we have to in order to save our own necks, regardless of what God has said. It will cause us to do our own thing and not regard the counsel and direction of the Lord, leading us to destruction.

This indeed is true in the case of Saul. It almost appears unimaginable to see that he is still experiencing the blessing of God, even after he has dishonored God (I Samuel 14:47, 48). He accomplished great deeds, like conquering the Amalekites, and saving Israel from previous conquerors, yet he would not see that his success was not because of him, but because of God's supernatural provision. God was allowing success for the sake of the people, not for Saul.

In chapter 15, verse 2, we see another act of disobedience. Through Samuel, Saul is informed that God is getting ready to settle accounts with the nation of Amalek for refusing to allow the Israelites to cross their territory when they came from Egypt. His implicit instructions are to destroy everything, including all humans and animals. Why did God command something like this? The Amalekites were a band of guerrilla terrorists. They lived by attacking other nations and carrying off their wealth and families. They had been the first to attack the Israelites as they entered the Promised Land, and they continued to raid Israelite camps at every opportunity. God knew that the Israelites could never live peaceably in Canaan (the Promised Land) as long as the Amalekites existed. He also knew that their corrupt, idolatrous, sacrilegious practices would threaten Israel's relationship with Him. Many of these surrounding nations, including Amalek, suffered from social diseases because of their sexual practices, including homosexuality and bestiality.

Saul, indeed, did conquer the Amalekites. But, even after having been warned by Samuel not to take anything, rather to destroy everything, he took the best of the sheep and oxen and the fattest of the lambs. In fact, he took everything that appealed to him (I Samuel 15:9). They destroyed only what was worthless or of poor quality. Can you imagine doing the total opposite of what God said to do? But Saul's selfish drive did not stop there. When Samuel found out that Saul had again disobeyed God, he began to search for him. Only to find, the next day, Saul had gone to Mt. Carmel to set himself a monument. His pride had raised him to the heights of selfishness and disobedience. Dishonest people soon begin to believe the lies they construct around themselves. They lose their ability to see the difference between telling the truth and lying.

By doing this, a person alienates himself further and further from God. Notice what Saul said in I Samuel 15:13 in the Living Bible; he claimed, "I have carried out the Lord's command." What a lie! Samuel immediately reproves him and Saul makes two excuses. First he says, "My troops demanded that I keep the best," and then he says, "I'm going to sacrifice them to the Lord." This is comparable to saying, "The people told me to steal the money to put it in the offering plate."

Perhaps we have one of the greatest truths and most famous verses in the Old Testament in the words of Samuel's response to Saul in I Samuel 15:22, 23. Samuel says, "Has the Lord as much pleasure in your burnt offerings and sacrifice as in your obedience? Obedience is far better than sacrifice. He is much more interested in your listening to Him than in your offering the fat of rams to Him. For rebellion is as bad as the sin of witchcraft, and stubbornness is as bad as worshipping idols. And now, because you have rejected the word of Jehovah, he has rejected you from being king." Saul's pride had destroyed him.

"Pride goeth before destruction, and a haughty spirit before a fall" (Proverbs 16:18). It is more important to follow God's Word than any other thing in life. Saul's life is a lesson in what not to do. He was rejected because of his stubbornness and pride. Humble yourself before God that He may exalt you in due season.

Things Are Not Always As They Appear

RE: I Samuel 15, 16

We have seen in the life of Saul that his leadership abilities did not match the expectations created by his appearance. First impressions were really deceiving, especially because Saul's appearance contradicted his qualities and abilities (I Samuel 9:2). Saul was the ideal visual image of a king. His dedication and commitment to the Lord and the words he was given did not match up to his appearance. During his reign, Saul had great success when he obeyed God. His greatest failures resulted from acting on his own. Saul had the raw materials to be a good leader for Israel at that time. He possessed a good appearance, valiant courage, and he was a man of action. Saul acted too many times on his own, however, and eventually cancelled his appointment as king of Israel.

I Samuel 15:24–30 shows that Saul was more concerned about what others would think of him than what the Lord would think of him. No religious ceremony, no sacrifice, no appearance, and no outward show could change the rebellion of his heart. A sacrifice was a ritual transaction between man and God that physically demonstrated a relationship between them. If the person's heart was not truly repentant, or if he did not truly love God, the sacrifice was a hollow ritual. Being religious, going to church, praying, and giving to charity are not enough if we do not act out of a heart of love toward God. Even though Saul looked the part from the outside, God knew his heart. Rebellion and stubbornness were serious sins; God put them in the same category as witchcraft and idol worship.

In the New Testament, we see an interesting contrast of two individuals who seem to be engaging in the same act of repentance. Their names are Judas and Peter. Judas had been used of Satan to finger out Jesus to a rejecting crowd. A man who had been trained alongside of eleven other men to cast out devils, heal the sick, and preach the kingdom of God had now denied and rejected Jesus (Luke 9:1, 2). It is notable that when the guards finally took Jesus and bound Him to take Him away, Judas felt sorry for what he had done (Matthew 26:47–51). The Living Bible states in Matthew 27:3, "Judas changed his mind and deeply regretted what he had done, and brought back the money to the chief priest [30 pieces of silver] trying to drop his charges against Jesus." Judas was acting very much like Saul. They did their own thing, and then seeing the outcome, felt sorry. True repentance means we not only feel sorry for what we do; but we turn from the things we have done to follow the right course.

Peter was another one who denied and rejected Jesus. His motive is also found in Matthew 26. Peter's life was filled with momentary failures. It was also filled with an honest heart of compassion and love for Jesus. Jesus had prophesied his denial and it infuriated Peter. When finally it came to pass and Peter realized what he had done, he wept bitterly. It was not only an outward show of emotion, but also a true repentant heart. Feeling remorseful, Judas went out and killed himself, while Peter, changing his ways, went back and was restored.

We see a similar contrast in I Samuel 16:1 as we read the Old Testament story of Saul and David, the next Bible character we are about to meet. Now that God has rejected Saul, Samuel is commissioned by God to take His horn of oil and go anoint a new king. God sent Samuel to Jesse's house.

For fear of Saul finding out and killing him, the Lord told him to take a heifer and set up a sacrifice and call Jesse and his sons to come. When they began to come, Samuel looked at Eliab, the eldest son, and said he was the one (I Samuel 16:6). Saul had been tall and handsome.

He was impressive looking. Samuel may have been trying to find some-one who looked like Saul to be the next king. God speaks to Samuel in I Samuel 16:7 in the Living Bible, saying, "Don't judge by a man's face or height," The King James says, "Man looks on the outward appearance, but God looketh upon the heart." God sees what we can't see.

Samuel marched all of Jesse's sons before him and each time the Lord would say no. Finally, one son was left, David. He was the youngest and was tending sheep, and Jesse called him in. David was just a young boy, trained only to tend sheep, and God said, he's the one—anoint him!

What a lesson to learn. We must never look on people and judge them. God knows the heart. We will find out in further meditations that David was far from perfect. He made many mistakes, some seemingly greater than Saul. But, like Peter, he had a heart after God's own heart, and Saul, like Judas, did not. God sees beyond what we are capable of seeing.

A Lesson in Contrasts

RE: I Samuel 16

Saul, at this time, has no knowledge of David's anointing by the prophet Samuel to be king. In fact, Saul was still legally the king, but God was preparing David for his future responsibilities. I Samuel 16:13 tells us the anointing oil that Samuel poured over David's head was a symbol of holiness. It was used to set people apart for God's service. Each king and priest of Israel was anointed with oil. This commissioned them as God's representatives to the nation.

It is amazing to note that almost simultaneously, in two different locations, while the prophet was anointing David king, the Bible says the Spirit of the Lord left Saul, and an evil spirit, allowed by the Lord, came upon Saul. What a contrast! Notice that first the Spirit of the Lord departed. His anointing to be king had been annulled because of his rebellion, disobedience, and pride. From the beginning of Genesis 6:3, we found out through Noah that God said, "My Spirit shall not always strive with man."

As Saul's aides watched what had happened to this once mighty warrior and general, now filled with fear and depression, they immediately realized what had happened and suggested a help to him. They told him they would find a good harpist to play for him whenever the tormenting spirit bothered him. They believed the harp music would quiet him and he would be well. One of them said he knew a young fellow in

Bethlehem, the son of a man named Jesse, who not only plays the harp well, but also is handsome, brave, strong, and wise. So, they sent for him and Jesse responded by not only sending David, his son, the one they asked for, but also a young goat, food, and wine on a donkey. Just imagine it! Saul has no idea who this David really is. All he knows is that whenever he is tormented, depressed, and fearful, this young man plays the harp and the evil spirit departs. Brilliantly devised by the Holy Spirit, David is gaining insight and learning, with firsthand information, about being a king.

When we are committed to God's plan for our lives, He will guide us into His perfect will (Psalm 37:4, 5).

You Need To Know Who You Are

RE: I Samuel 17

Even though David had been anointed by Samuel to be king and an evil spirit had entered Saul, indicating that the anointing had been taken off of him, David was not going to be king yet for many years. God so arranged it that David would be able to spend time in the king's palace, learning the life of a king, while playing his harp to soothe Saul during the times of his awful fears and depressions. It doesn't seem, though, that David stayed in the king's palace all the time. We will see, in this little narrative, that he was still living in his father's house much of the time.

In our text, I Samuel 17:2, 3, the Philistines again mustered their army for battle against Israel. The two armies faced each other on opposite sides of hills with a valley in between. It seems that often, an army tried to avoid the high cost of battle by putting its strongest warrior against the strongest warrior of its enemy. This avoided great bloodshed. This was the case during this battle. The Philistines had a warrior named Goliath who measured more than nine feet in height. What an imposing figure to Israel. He stood and shouted across the valley to the Israelites in verses 8–10, "Do you need an army to settle this? I will represent the Philistines and you choose someone to represent you, and we will settle this in single combat. If your man is able to kill me, then we will be your slaves. But if I kill him, then you must be our slaves! I defy the armies of Israel! Send me a man who will fight with me!"

The Bible explains that when Saul and his army heard this, they were dismayed and frightened. Three of David's older brothers had already volunteered for duty in Saul's army to fight the Philistines. David was now back at Jesse's house tending his father's sheep; this shows the part-time basis of David's work in Saul's palace. For forty days, Goliath strutted before the armies of Israel twice a day, morning and evening. There was no one bold enough to match up to him. There was no one bold enough to realize who was on Israel's side.

One day Jesse tells David to take a bushel of roasted grain and loaves of bread to his brothers. He tells him to take cheese for their captain, and to find out how his brothers are getting along. He asks David to bring back a letter from them. David went on his way the next morning with the gifts. When he arrived at the outskirts of the camp, the army was leaving for the battlefield to face the Philistines. He ran to his brothers to find out how they were. As he talked with them, he saw Goliath, the giant, step out from the Philistine troops to shout his challenge to the army of Israel, as he had done for the previous forty days. Just as before, when they saw him and heard him, they ran away frightened. They asked one another, "Have you seen the giant? He has insulted the entire army of Israel. And have you heard the huge reward the king has offered to any one who kills him? He'll give him one of his daughters and his whole family will be exempt from paying taxes."

When David heard this, he asked if this offer was so and then said, "Who is this heathen Philistine that he is allowed to defy the armies of the living God?" (I Samuel 17:26). When David's brothers heard him talking that way, they began to criticize him.

"What are you doing here anyway?" they said. "Aren't you supposed to be taking care of Dad's sheep?" Eliab even accused David of being prideful and having a "naughty heart," and exclaimed that he was only agitating them so that he could see the fight while he was there.

After conferring with several others, King Saul heard that David wanted to go up to fight the giant. The king sent for him, and when he came, he said to Saul, "Let no man's heart fail because of him," or, "Don't worry about him, I'll take care of this Philistine" (I Samuel 17:32).

Saul said, "How can a kid like you fight with a man like him?" David persisted, telling him about his experiences in his father's fields tending sheep when he killed a lion and a bear. So, he finally consented, hearing David say, "The Lord who saved me from the claws and teeth of the lion and the bear will save me from this Philistine."

Saul wanted David to wear his armor. However, when he tried it, he found he could hardly move. He took it off, went to a nearby stream, and chose five smooth stones for his sling. David knew something about His God and was confident about what was going to happen. Goliath had overwhelming odds in his favor, and a sure advantage over David from a human standpoint, but Goliath didn't realize that in fighting David, he was fighting God. David not only knew his God, he knew who he was in God.

Confessing Who You Are

RE: I Samuel 17

In this text, we find David, a young shepherd boy, out on the battlefield hearing the threats of the enemy, Goliath, and becoming angry at what he hears. He also sees that no one is brave enough to do anything about his threat. He volunteers, knowing that God is with him. I believe David could still sense the fresh anointing of the oil Samuel poured on him. He knew something about his God and did not feel intimidated at all by the giant's threat. It is fair enough proof that David's anointing was real since he testified of killing a lion and a bear with his hands. That does not "just happen!"

As David approached the giant with his sling and five stones, Goliath began to sneer at him in contempt. He mocked, "What do you think I'm a dog that you come at me with a stick?"

Watch closely the reply David gives in I Samuel 17:45, 46, when he says, "You come to me with a sword and a spear, but I come to you in the name of the Lord of the armies of heaven and of Israel, the very God you have defied. Today the Lord will conquer you, and will kill you and cut off your head, and then I will give the dead bodies of your men to the birds and wild animals. And the whole world will know that there is a God in Israel." Now listen to these words from verse 47, the confession of David's faith; he says, "And Israel will learn that the Lord does not depend on weapons to fulfill his plans. He works without regard to human means! He will give you to us!" David did not speak the problem; he spoke the answer! He did not speak fear—he spoke faith!

Here's a little formula that will help you do the same thing. When you know who God is, what He has, and what He can do, you will know who *you* are, what *you* have, and what *you* can do, then you will know who Satan is, what he does *not* have, and what he *cannot* do! David's hope was in God. Confession is agreeing with God. It is not creating something that does not exist. David spoke what he believed and believed what he spoke. The result of Goliath being killed was the confidence of God, and what David believed and said (Psalm 116:10; II Corinthians 4:13).

We can experience the same results. We must stop praying or talking the problem, and start praying and talking the answer. We cannot continue to accentuate the problem and then expect victory. Our victory is in our mouth! This is a principle and law established at creation! God spoke, and the world came into existence; the pattern of confession is throughout the Word of God. Each of us began our Christian walk by believing in our hearts and confessing with our mouths that Jesus is Lord. Our Christian walk is to be lived with that same action; every day we must speak what God says! Remember what we recently studied concerning Jonathan. (For a good review of what happens by saying the wrong things, study Numbers 14:26–28.) At the beginning, David was criticized for what he said. In the end, he prevailed and his faith brought down Goliath. Thank God we can do the same and bring down the Devil by standing boldly on God's Word, believing in our hearts and confessing with our mouths (Hebrews 13:5, 6).

The Consequences
of Jealousy

RE: I Samuel 18

Proverbs 6:34 says, "Jealousy is the rage of a man: therefore he will not spare in the day of vengeance."

Saul has just seen and experienced an incredible sight. David has come off the battlefield successfully, having slain Goliath and the armies of the Philistines. David's spiritual boldness and strength in God was now highly visible, not only to Saul, but to all of Israel. Saul wanted to find out more about David and he began to ask questions, first of people around him, then of David himself. Saul decided to no longer let David return home, but to keep him constantly around him. He became Saul's special assistant, carrying out special assignments until finally, he was appointed commander of his troops, much to the delight of the army and general public alike (I Samuel 18:5).

But something happened to terribly upset Saul. Returning from one of their many victories over the Philistines, David and his army heard the celebration of the women coming out from all the towns along the way, singing and dancing for joy with tambourines and cymbals. They were singing this song, "Saul has slain his thousands and David his ten thousands."

This incensed Saul. He said (The Amplified Bible), "They credit David with ten thousands and me with only thousands. What more can he have but the kingdom?" Or, in other words, "Next they'll want him to be king." Notice this key verse in I Samuel 18:9, (The Amplified Bible), which says, "And Saul jealously eyed David from that day forward."

Whatever appreciation Saul had for David because of his mighty victories over the enemy had now turned to jealousy. In I Samuel 18:11, Saul, in a jealous rage, attempts to kill David with his javelin as David plays his harp for him. In fact, this happened twice, and each time, David evaded him. How amazing! Only God could make someone "evade" a javelin. You don't just duck from a weapon of that caliber!

The Scripture says in verse 12, "Saul was afraid of David because the Lord was with him but had departed from Saul." He could not live with himself knowing that God was no longer with him. This jealous spirit that was now in him would eventually drive him to try to destroy David. Jealousy may not seem to be a major sin, but in reality, it is one step short of murder. It begins by destroying a person on the inside, and then it manifests itself in harmful actions, and, if not corrected, may eventually lead to death. James 3:16 says, "For where envying and strife is, there is confusion and every evil work."

It is so important to keep right attitudes on the inside, or a wrong attitude will produce every evil work. Man looks on the outward appearance, while God is always looking at our hearts. If our attitudes are wrong, we can expect to fail. The reward of maintaining a right attitude and a pure heart before God cannot be compared to the agony of giving in to a jealous one.

Loyalty, the Missing Ingredient

RE: I Samuel 19, 20

Saul, now constantly troubled by an evil spirit, and in realization that there is a special anointing on David, is enraged, and attempts again to kill David. I Samuel 18:12 best describes one of the main reasons why the anger of Saul was so great. "And Saul was afraid of David, because the Lord was with him, and was departed from Saul." What a horrible situation to be confronted with! Imagine having to face the fact that the Lord is no longer with you! Thank God for His Word, and a new covenant based on better promises! In I Samuel 18:14, it is clear that the Lord was with David; "And David behaved himself wisely in all of his ways; and the Lord was with him."

The intense spirit of jealousy had now driven Saul to try to murder David to get him out of his way. I Samuel 19:1 opens with Saul urging his aides and his son Jonathan to assassinate David. Notice what it says, "But Jonathan, because of his close friendship with David, told him what his father was planning." Jonathan went on to tell David to hide himself, and in the meanwhile, he would talk to his father, Saul, to find out what was really on his mind. In essence, Jonathan was disobeying his father; however, we must recognize that Saul was deliberately breaking the law of God, and Jonathan would not follow this murderous plot, which was in opposition to the plan and purpose of God. Remember in I Samuel

18:3–4, Jonathan and David had come into covenant with each other and an immediate bonding of love came upon them. Jonathan swore to be his blood brother and sealed the pact by giving him his robe, sword, bow, and belt. They had entered into blood covenant together. Now, in I Samuel 19:4–6, Jonathan convinces his father not to kill David, and Saul vows that he will not be killed. Sure of this, Jonathan brought David back to Saul, and things seemed to return to normal once again. As a matter of fact, shortly after this whole incident, David was directly responsible for having slaughtered the Philistines who, once again, had come against Israel.

Saul remained pacified for a short while; but, one day, as David sat with Saul, playing his harp, the tormenting spirit attacked Saul once again. Saul got his spear in his hand and hurled it at David in an attempt to kill him. Once again David dodged it (once again, supernaturally), and fled into the night, leaving the spear imbedded in the timber of the wall. Dominated and controlled by this oppressive and tormenting demon, Saul sent his troops to watch David's house with orders to kill him when he came out in the morning. But, enveloped in the hand of the Lord, and with the help of Michal, his wife, David escaped through a window.

Now on the run, David goes to find Jonathan and asks him why his father is out to kill him. Jonathan is still not convinced that this is so, telling David, "My father tells me even the littlest thing. I'm sure he would have told me about any plan to kill you."

David responds, "Your father knows perfectly well about our friendship, and that's why he hasn't told you anything. But I am one step away from death." David then reveals a plan of how Jonathan will secretly tell him what is going on as he is hiding in the field (I Samuel 20:5–9).

It was during this conversation that we have one of the most incredible scenes of brotherly love and spoken loyalty seen in the entire Bible. Jonathan promises (covenants) that he will fulfill the plan that David has made to protect him. He already knows that he won't be the king in Israel, but that David will, and he tells him, "May the Lord be with you as he used to be with my father. Remember you must demonstrate the love and kindness of the Lord not only to me during my own lifetime, but also to my children" (I Samuel 20:13, 14). So Jonathan made a covenant with the family of David, and David swore to it, knowing there was a terrible curse against him and his descendants if he was unfaithful to his promise. Jonathan loved David as much as he loved himself; and this love would allow him to become increasingly responsible for saving David's life and fulfilling the plan of God. David, in future days as king, would repay Jonathan's loyalty and his part of the covenant back.

Loyalty is one of life's most priceless qualities. It is the most selfless part of love. To be loyal, you cannot live only for yourself; and often, commitments to satisfy the person being shown loyalty to far surpass in importance and priority the commitments we make to ourselves. Loyal people not only stand by their commitments, they are willing to suffer for them. Jonathan is a shining example of loyalty. Sometimes he was forced to deal with a conflict of loyalties—to his father Saul or to his friend David. His solution for that conflict teaches us both how to be loyal and what must guide our loyalty. In Jonathan, truth always guided loyalty. Jonathan realized his source of truth was the God who demanded his ultimate loyalty. The truth of God's Word is the ultimate choice of where our loyalty stands. With this in mind, our decisions will always be much clearer. God's Word in us is more important than any decision in life that is made from a human relationship. Oh that more of us could learn Bible loyalty and covenant relations!

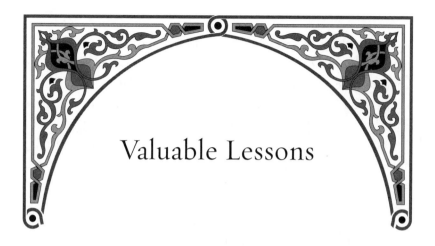

Valuable Lessons

RE: I Samuel 20—26

There are many lessons that we learn as we peruse through the closing chapters of I Samuel and follow the life of David as he is running from Saul. We have found that an evil spirit has troubled Saul so much that a spirit of jealousy has driven him to pursue David and kill him. Because of this, David is in constant hiding from Saul. Many of the Psalms were written as David was experiencing the terror, discouragement, and fear of the contract Saul had placed on his life. David ran from city to city and from cave to cave to avoid the challenge dispensed by Saul.

In I Samuel 24, David and his men are hiding in a cave. David had the opportunity to kill Saul as he entered a cave, but although Saul was in a state of sin and rebellion against God, David respected the position he held as God's anointed king. He knew that he would one day be king, and that God would be the one to do it, and he did not want to risk reaping the result of killing Saul. Psalm 75:6 says, "Promotion does not come from the east or west, but from above."

If David assassinated Saul, he would be setting a precedent for his own opponents to remove him some day. It was God that placed Saul on the throne, as a result of Israel's request, and it would be God who would remove him. Romans 13:1–7 teaches us that God has placed the government leaders in power. We may not know why, but like David, we are to respect the positions and roles of those in authority. There is one exception, however. Since God is our highest authority, we should not allow a leader to force us to violate God's law (Acts 4:19). The disciples chose to follow God's Word about preaching the gospel and healing the sick rather than the opinion of the crowd and the laws of the land.

In another instance in I Samuel 26, David once again has Saul at his disposal. He and a servant, Abishai, sneak into a camp where Saul is with his 3,000 elite troops. With the opportunity to kill Saul, Abishai tells David that God has put his enemy within his power this time for sure. "Let me go and put that spear through him," he pleads.

"No," David said. "Who will remain innocent after attacking the Lord's chosen king?" The strongest moral decisions are the ones we make before temptation strikes. David was determined to follow God's plan, not his own. Even when the circumstances seemed to make this feasible, David did not want to run ahead of God's timing, though he had been in a severe struggle. What a valuable lesson to learn. Let's let God fulfill His plan His way!

Two Lives in Contrast

RE: I Samuel 20—31

When Saul had crossed the line of disobedience for the last time, and the anointing of the Holy Spirit had been removed from him, Samuel, the prophet, found another king in Jesse's house named David. It was going to take approximately sixteen years for David to reach the throne, and much suffering and pain. This obsession Saul had to kill David seemed to be the only thing on his mind. Scripture records many times that David had several opportunities, while in Saul's pursuit, to kill Saul, but he respected Saul's position and would not tamper with it.

In our last meditation, we saw how David was going to wait for God's time. The book of I Samuel, chapters 20–31, is filled with many stories about these two lives in contrast. As Saul grew worse, David, through a life of struggle, grew stronger. As we close this study of David and Saul, please note the contrast in their lives. It's interesting to note that both of them were far from perfect. The contrast was that David had a heart after God, while Saul was more interested in what people thought about him.

Our only concern should be to please the Lord. The Scripture says in Proverbs 16:7, "When a man's ways please the Lord, he maketh even his enemies to be at peace with him." Saul had to learn the hard way. If we refuse to listen to the Lord when He speaks to us, we will get results that we may not be very happy with. Proverbs 1:24–26 says, "Because I have called and ye refused, I have stretched out my hand, and no man regarded; But ye have set at naught all my counsel, and would none of my reproof: I will also laugh at your calamity; I will mock when your fear cometh;" I don't want to ever get to that place! I want to choose to always listen to the Lord in everything that He says. As Proverbs 3:13 says, "Happy is the man that findeth wisdom," and Proverbs 3:16 says, "Length of days is in her right hand, and in her left hand riches and honor." That's where I want to be, don't you?

David was God's kind of king. Saul was man's kind of king. David was forgiving; Saul was unforgiving. David was honest and repentant. Saul, as proven when confronted, was a liar. These are just a few comparisons and contrasts of the character of a man after God's own heart and a man who is not. I think it is very clear who we should imitate.

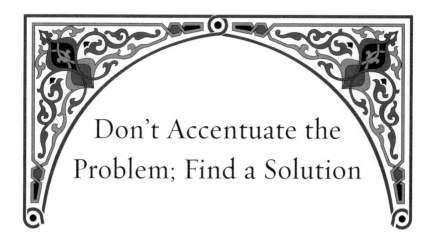

Don't Accentuate the Problem; Find a Solution

RE: I Samuel 26–30

After his final encounter with Saul (I Samuel 26), having had the opportunity to kill him, David fled from Saul again, fearing for his life. He spared Saul's life, but wisely, he did not trust him at all. For the second time, David fled to Philistine territory, to the city of Gath, which was under the leadership of Achish, one of the five rulers of the Philistines (I Samuel 27:2, 3). David eventually left the city of Gath and moved south to Ziklag. There in the south, he and his men conducted guerrilla raids among the Geshurites, the Girzites, and the Amalekites, who were known for their surprise attacks and cruel treatment of innocent people. These desert tribes were a great threat to both the Philistines and the Jews. David and his men would recover the spoils of the war, including the sheep, oxen, donkeys, camels, and whatever else they had. Achish, believing that David was now hated by Israel for living among the Philistines, actually thought he could stay there forever (I Samuel 27:12).

Soon the leaders of the Philistines gathered together and mobilized their troops to fight the Israelites. David and his troops were marching in the rear. Personally, I do not believe that they were going to literally fight Israel. It could very well have been that they would try to defeat the Philistines from the rear. The leaders began to recognize this, saying of David, "Isn't he the one that the women of Israel sang about in their dances saying, 'Saul has slain his thousands and David his ten thousands?'" To eliminate the possibility of David turning on them, they sent him away. He headed back to Ziklag, while the rest of the army pursued to Jezreel to attack Israel (I Samuel 29:1–5).

Three days later, when David and his men arrived home to Ziklag, they found that the Amalekites had raided the city and burned it to the ground, carrying off all the women and the children (I Samuel 30:1, 2). David and his men looked at the ruins, realized what happened, and wept until, as the King James Version puts it, they "had no more power to weep." David became seriously worried because his men, in bitter grief for their children, began talking of killing him. Think of David's life! Ever since he was anointed king, unbelievable things began to happen. While on the battlefield with Goliath, he was the only one brave and confident enough to face the giant, while his fearful family mocked him and accused him of being proud. The next years of his life were spent with King Saul in constant pursuit to kill him, making his life one of hiding and running. Now, his own men were threatening to kill him, believing that the misfortune of Ziklag were his fault! Listen to this exciting verse from I Samuel 30:6, in the Amplified Bible, which says, "But David encouraged and strengthened himself in the Lord."

What do we do in the time of trouble? Do we panic? Do we run? Do we complain? If we are going to follow the example of David, then we will not panic, we will not run, and we will not complain! It is very evident that real men and women of God don't run *from* God, they run *to* God!

All of those hard years, David's strength and help were from God. He had no other place to go but to the Lord. His courage was in God! His strength was in God! His solution was in God! It was not time to accentuate, discuss, or attempt to resolve the problem. It was time for an answer, and the only hope of an answer he had was God. In Psalm 18:2, David says, "The Lord is my rock, my fortress, my deliverer, my God, my strength in whom I will trust!" Our strength does not come from anyone or anything other than God. Talking about the problem or blaming someone else will only make matters worse. We have to recognize and submit to the fact that God really does have everything under control.

As David inquired of the Lord, asking, "Shall I chase them? Will I catch them?" The Lord replied, "Pursue, for thou shalt surely overtake them, and without fail recover all." They went on their way, and the Lord brought them to a servant who was left to die. They fed and restored him to health, and as God had promised, He used this man to lead David and his troops to the Amalekites encampment. As the Amalekites were dancing and celebrating over the vast amount of spoil they had taken, David and his troops interrupted their party and slaughtered them throughout the night and the following day. When they were through conquering, they took back everything that had been stolen, including their children and wives. They recovered all. We will get God's results when we inquire of the Lord! He is our refuge and our strength, a very present help in the time of trouble.

Good Beginnings Don't Guarantee Good Endings

RE: I Samuel 31

The last chapter of I Samuel records the tragic death of Israel's first king, Saul. Saul had an auspicious beginning. It was this young, handsome man, who, although chosen to be the first king of Israel, throughout his life chose most often to take matters into his own hands rather than consulting the Lord. The life of Samuel, the man who judged Israel before Saul, was characterized by consistency and obedience, as well as a deep desire for God's will. Saul's life was characterized by inconsistency, disobedience, and self-will. Samuel was dedicated to God; Saul was dedicated to himself. Even though the anointing of the Holy Spirit came upon Saul (I Samuel 10:6–10), he was not consistent in his faith to the Lord. He tried to please God with "spirits of religiosity," but true spirituality requires a lifetime of consistent obedience and submission to the Word of the Lord. Heroic spiritual lives are built by stacking days of obedience on top of one another. Like a brick, each obedient act is small in itself, but in time the acts will pile up and a huge wall of strong character will be built as a great defense against temptation. We must strive for consistent obedience each day.

In I Corinthians 9:24–27, the Apostle Paul gives an example of a person running a race to illustrate consistency. He states that winning a race requires purpose and discipline. It also takes hard work and self-denial to prepare for the demands ahead. Paul further states that any athlete who desires to win will strive for the prize with much preparation, going through all these struggles and training just to win a blue ribbon or a silver cup. How much more, then, should we train spiritually, enduring hardships and submitting to the Word of God, to win a heavenly reward that will never disappear? I think the strongest statement Paul makes is the final verse of the chapter, verse 27, when he says, "But I keep under my body, and bring it into subjection: lest that by any means, when I have preached to others, I myself should be a castaway." He explains that after preaching a message of discipline and endurance, if he himself didn't submit to it, he would be unfit. Remember—it is not how fast you start the race; it's what happens at the finish line. Saul's life is a classic example of a reject. The Bible declares that Jesus is the author and the finisher of our faith. Let's strive on. Read Proverbs 1:20–33 for a stirring testimony from Solomon, and a reminder of what not to do.

Bad Habits Are Hard To Break

RE: II Samuel 1–3

David was a man of great faith in God. He had waited many years for God to fulfill His promise to him. In I Samuel, we read of Saul's pursuit of David to kill him. We learned of David's struggles, hiding in caves and living for many years in enemy territory, or in the barren wilderness south and east of Jerusalem. I believe there were plenty of times when David wondered if God was really there. Many of those times of wondering are recorded in the Psalms. Now, a victim of his own sin, Saul is dead, and in II Samuel, we are going to see David's many years of faith and determination rewarded.

David and his men were still living in Ziklag, a Philistine city, when news came to them that Saul had been killed on the battlefield. David and his men mourned and fasted the entire day. Even though Saul had put David and his men through the proverbial ringer, there was true sorrow over the loss of their king. A new struggle was about to arise.

David moved back to Judah and sent word to those loyal to Saul that Judah had anointed him king. He explained that they had received him as their leader, and told them to receive him also. He promised them that he would be kind to them (II Samuel 2:6). While this was happening, Abner, Saul's Commander in Chief, crowned one of Saul's sons, Ishbosheth, king. Judah had already pledged allegiance to David, so once again, the kingdom was going to be divided. Abner and Saul's sons and families had learned terrible habits from Saul. They knew the struggle between Saul and David, and they had become the products of what they saw and heard. Proverbs 13:21 says, "Curses chase sinners, while blessings chase the righteous." How sad to see that Saul's family was now so terribly astray. As a result, Israel was divided and there was constant tension between the north and the south, until eventually, war broke out among the opposing groups. The curses of Saul were now upon his followers, but the blessings were going to follow David because of his heart after God.

II Samuel 3:1 shows that a long war began between Saul's followers and David's followers, but notice that the Living Bible says, "David grew stronger and stronger, and the house of Saul grew weaker and weaker."

How true Proverbs 13:21 is, and how important it is not to follow bad habits. I want blessings to chase me, and the Word declares that they will if I remain righteous. However, if I live in unrepentant sin, curses will chase me. We must develop good habits that are hard to break!

David's Ultimate Anointing

RE: II Samuel 4

The first few chapters of II Samuel reveal much bloodshed as a result of power struggles between the divided leadership of Israel. Ishbosheth, the appointed king of Israel, was really a fearful, incapable leader who was chosen merely on the basis of being the son of the former king. His short reign was one spent in constant war.

A decision was finally made to unite the north and south (Israel and Judah) into one kingdom. When Ishbosheth heard that Abner (a former close friend of Saul) was dead, his courage failed, and the Israelites were dismayed. Probably unaware that the Spirit of God was leading them, Rechab and Baanah (brothers that led raiding bands) went to Ishbosheth's door pretending to deliver wheat. They killed him, beheaded him, and brought his head to David. In spite of all of David's heartache, he still mourned these deaths, especially Ishbosheth's. Although David had been severely persecuted and pursued by Saul, he maintained respect for Saul's son Ishbosheth because of the office he stood in. In II Samuel 5:1, representatives of all the tribes of Israel came to David at Hebron, where he had reigned as king of Judah for seven years. When they arrived, they pledged loyalty to him. Finally, because David had remained steadfast, Samuel's prophetic words, spoken to him as a young boy, were indeed coming to pass (I Samuel 16:13).

David was now 37 years old. For all of those years in between, David stood, waiting patiently for the fulfillment of God's promise. Whenever we feel pressured to achieve instant results and success, we must remember David's patience. Proverbs 3:5, 6 in the Living Bible says, "If you want favor with God and man, and a reputation for good judgment and common sense, then trust the Lord completely, don't even trust yourself. In everything you do, put God first, and he will direct you and crown your efforts with success!" It had been a long wait, and there were many dark days, but now the wait was over! I Samuel 5:3 tells us, "They crowned him king of Israel." This was the third time he had been crowned. First, he was privately anointed by Samuel (I Samuel 16:13), then he was crowned king over Judah (II Samuel 2:4), and now, finally, he was crowned king of Israel. When he was on the run, life looked bleak, but now God's promise was fulfilled. He took his troops of 2,100 to Jerusalem to overcome the Jebusites who lived there. Again, God gave him victory. He would rule in this city for thirty-three more years (forty years total). David was now at the place where he could walk in his ultimate anointing.

They that put their trust in the Lord shall never be ashamed! David is a testimony to this, and we can be too.

Who Gets the Glory?

RE: II Samuel 5

I Corinthians 1:31 (Living Bible) says, "If anyone is going to boast, let him boast only of what the Lord has done."

Life on the run had been very hard for David, but he had learned many lessons. One of the most valuable lessons he had learned was to trust God, no matter what was going on around him. Finally, after many years of struggle, David became king over all of God's people, and his good attitude had not changed. He continued to rely on God. This is so beautifully illustrated in II Samuel 5. David had a heart after God. He realized that his help and strength came from God. Success would not spoil him as it had many others.

When David came to Jerusalem, (Zion, the city of David), the Philistines heard that David had been crowned king, and they tried to capture him by spreading themselves across the valley of Rephaim (I Samuel 5:18). Notice what the Scriptures say of David; "David inquired of the Lord." Thank God we can go to God and talk with Him. But not only do we talk to Him, He answers us back! David said, "Shall I go up and fight against them? Will you defeat them?" Then, in I Samuel 5:19, he said, "Deliver them into my hands," and the Lord replied, "Yes, go ahead, for I will give them to you." So David went out and fought with them and defeated them. Let us see what he did next.

As king, he could very well have gloated in the glory of the victory, heaping praise on himself for it. He was smart enough to realize that his strength came from his God. The Living Bible says in I Samuel 5:20 that David proclaimed, "The Lord did it." David fought battles the way the Lord had instructed him to. In fact, in the same chapter, the Philistines came back and started all over again. Unmoved, David did what he always had done; he inquired of the Lord. God honored His Word again, giving David the plans on how to defeat them. These are three important things we are to do that David did:

1. Ask the Lord what to do.
2. Follow the instructions.
3. Give God the glory.

Each of these three steps is equally important. We can err in life by ignoring any one of them. David's life was filled with success as long as he honored God and gave Him the glory. Our lives will be equally successful if we do the same.

The Ark of the Covenant, the Glory of God

RE: II Samuel 6

After David's leadership resulted in two great victories over the Philistines in the valley of Rephaim, he mobilized 30,000 willing men to retrieve the ark of the Lord. David recognized the great significance of the ark as the earthly throne of Jehovah, God of Israel. I Samuel 4:4 describes Jehovah enthroned between the cherubims. It was there that the Lord Almighty manifested His presence. It was a sure sign of God's presence with Israel. During the entire reign of Saul, the ark of God had not been considered. In I Chronicles 13:3 (Living Bible), David said, "Let us bring back the ark of God, for we have been neglecting it ever since Saul became king." The neglect of the ark symbolized Saul's reign and Israel's neglect for God. Now as a true theocratic king, David wished to acknowledge the Lord's kingship and rule over both himself and the people by restoring the ark to a place of prominence in Israel. It was David's desire to remind the nation of its true foundation, Jehovah God. Neglecting those things that remind us of God will cause us to also neglect God. That is one of the reasons why the book of Hebrews encourages us not to "forsake the assembling of ourselves together." Without Him as the center of our lives, life itself will not reach its highest potential. Remember the words of Moses in Exodus 33:15; "If your presence doesn't go with us, don't send us from here." Moses, in essence, had said, "We need You; without

You, we will not go anywhere." This depicted utter dependence on God. For so many years, Saul lacked this dependence and led Israel to lack it, but David, already dependent on God, was bringing this attitude back to Israel.

As the ark of God was returning, David made a major mistake. He failed to obey the instruction given in Exodus, which stated that the Levites were the only ones who could carry it. David had a new cart built, much like the one that the Philistines had when they took the ark in I Samuel 6:7. David's heart was right. He knew he had to bring back the ark, but he did not obey the instructions of the law, and as a result, there would be unfortunate, evil results.

David and the whole house of Israel were celebrating with singing and playing instruments. When they came to the threshing floor of Nacon, the oxen stumbled, and as the ark started to fall, a man named Uzzah reached out to catch it. Although Uzzah's intent may have been good, he violated the clear instructions that the Lord had given for the handling of the ark in Numbers 4:5, 6 and was stricken dead. It also seems very clear that Uzzah was not a Levite, and they were the only ones allowed to touch the ark of the Lord. At this important new beginning in Israel's life in submission to God's leadership, the Lord gave a vivid and shocking reminder to David and Israel. Those who claim to serve Him must acknowledge God's rule in absolute seriousness. Enthusiasm must be accompanied by obedience. Zeal for God without knowledge can be dangerous.

II Samuel 6:8 says that David was very angry that a well-meaning man had been killed, and that his plans for a joyous return of the ark had been spoiled. Now it was time to consider what had been done. He did not follow close instructions, and now fear and anger were building up inside him. Watch what happened next. This little incident will sum up what God can do in any life when His glory comes on a person.

In his anger and fear of the Lord (verse 9), David decided not to continue his journey with the ark to Israel, but to take it aside to the house of Obed-edom, a Gittite. The ark would remain in this man's house for three months. Look at what happens in II Samuel 6:11. The New International Version says, "The ark remained in the house of Obed-edom three months, and the Lord blessed him and his entire household." At first, this doesn't appear to be as significant as it really is, but if we look further, we will see the significance. First of all, the name "Obed-edom" means "servant of man." It is from the root word "bond slave servant." So, we can say this name really signified obedience. There is no better place for blessings to be than around obedience. Note also Josephus. Ancient Bible historians explain that this man was poor before the ark came, and all of a sudden he became rich and prosperous. It was almost like he had won the lottery! But his instant success was not by man—it was by God.

After hearing of this success story and allowing his anger to cool down, there is no doubt that David reconsidered his ways and prepared himself to bring the ark back—the way God wanted it returned. As they were coming into the city with the ark of the covenant, David danced with all his might to the sound of music and there was shouting from all of Israel. They set the ark in the midst of the tabernacle David had pitched, and there was great rejoicing. The manifest glory of God had finally returned; indeed, it was time to celebrate! God's visible presence was again among the people. Sacrifice and offerings were being made to the God of Israel. How wonderful that God has been given back His rightful place, willingly, by the people. The God of Covenant now, once again, is the respected King over Israel. We must never forget that without God, we are nothing! (John 15:5)

The Danger of a Critical Spirit

RE: II Samuel 6:20–23

Ephesians 4:29 says, "Let no corrupt communication proceed out of your mouth but that which is good to the use of edifying, that it may minister grace to the hearers." The Living Bible describes it as "unwholesome" or "worthless" talk.

It appears that we are living in a time in the history of man where there is a very critical spirit loosed on the earth. News reporters seem to specialize in "digging up the dirt." It seems that the more revealing and "juicy" the story is, the more publicity is given. While this is somewhat understandable to the world, it should be unheard of in the church and among God's people. It is so sad to see how Michal (Saul's daughter and David's wife) became so critical of David simply because he danced with joy before the ark of God as it was returning to Israel. She was so concerned with David's undignified actions (which, by the way, really weren't undignified) that she did not rejoice in the return of the ark. She emphasized the outward appearance while David emphasized the inward condition of his heart before God. He was willing to look foolish in the eyes of some in order to worship his Lord and his God.

It is a dangerous thing to criticize, particularly to criticize God's leaders. One of the more interesting Scriptures in the Bible is found in Jude 9. It says that even Michael, the archangel, when contending for the body of Moses with the Devil, would not bring a railing accusation against him. Jude was writing this to compare it with those who speak evil of dignities and speak things they don't even know (Jude 8–10). In II Peter 2:10–12, Peter repeats the same thing. He explains that those who accuse leaders walk after the flesh, and he goes on to say that those who are not afraid to bring railing accusations and speak evil of dignities will utterly perish in their own corruption.

Psalm 105:15 declares, "Touch not mine anointed, and do my prophets no harm." Backbiting and gossiping against leadership is dangerous! There are other incidents recorded in Scripture to show how true this is. Here are a few:

Miriam mocked Moses because he had a Cushite wife and then she was stricken with leprosy (Numbers 12).

Korah and his followers led the people of Israel against Moses' leadership in rebellion and were swallowed up by the earth (Numbers 16).

Young men mocked Elisha and laughed at his baldness and were then killed by bears (II Kings 2).

Hananiah contradicted Jeremiah's prophecies with false predictions and died two months later (Jeremiah 28).

Here in our text, Michal had contempt for David because he danced before the Lord. As a result, she lived her life in shame due to her barrenness.

We must speak the truth in love. We must only allow things that edify, exhort, and encourage to be spoken. May our speech always be seasoned with salt (Colossians 4:6).

Let Him That Standeth Take Heed

RE: II Samuel 11

As we read chapters 7–10 of II Samuel, we saw God using David to restore the united nation of Israel to peace. In chapter 7, we saw that God made covenant with David to bless his household for all future generations. In chapter 8, the king conquered all the surrounding nations. In chapter 9, he restored the son of Jonathan, Mephibosheth, by giving him the land that was in his family background through Saul, his grandfather. David did this because of his blood covenant with Jonathan. We see here the kind of heart that David had—a heart of grace and truth.

However, we will soon find (as depicted in chapter 11) that no matter how good we have been and how many good acts we have done, we must remain alert and on guard so we do not lapse into mediocrity—a result of not keeping the Word of God in our hearts. Chapter 10 describes Israel's fight with the Syrians and the Ammorites, and once again, how the Lord was with David to help him defeat his enemies.

After restoring the nation to peace, David's personal life becomes entangled in sin. Sometimes, success makes us very passive in maintaining our walk with God. I believe a key verse that hints to us why David placed himself in a position to fail is II Samuel 11:1 (New International Version), which says, "In the spring, at the time when kings go off to war, David sent Joab out with the king's men and the whole Israelite army."

David seemingly had abandoned his purpose by staying home from battle. It was during one of these nights at home when he couldn't sleep that he went for a walk on the palace roof. There he noticed a woman of unusual beauty taking a bath. In a time of weakness, David sent for this beautiful woman, Bathsheba, who was the wife of a soldier named Uriah. Bethsheba came, slept with David, and then, apparently several weeks later, sent word to him that she was pregnant. David had focused his attention on his own desires. When temptation came he looked into it, rather than turned from it. The Bible instructs us in I Peter 5:8 (The Living Bible) to "be alert, be careful, for attacks from Satan, your great enemy. He prowls around like a hungry, roaring lion, looking for some victim to tear apart. Stand firm when he attacks!" David could have chosen to stop and turn from evil at any stage along the way, but he chose not to.

Reading II Samuel 11, we find that when David heard that Bathsheba was pregnant, he sent for Uriah, Bathsheba's husband, to be brought home from the battlefield where Israel was fighting the Ammorites to make him sleep with his wife. David wanted Uriah to believe that the child to be born would be his. There was such loyalty in Uriah, that even though they brought him home to visit his wife, he would not leave the king's palace, but would remain loyal and faithful to stay at the gateway to the palace with the other servants of the king. When David found out, he called him and asked him why he didn't go home to his wife the night before after having been away so long. Uriah explained that the ark, the armies, the general (Joab), and his officers were camping in open fields. He asked why he should go home to drink, dine, and sleep with his wife while others were on the battlefield. So, David told him to stay in the palace that night. David's intention was not to be kind; his intention was to get him drunk and then perhaps he would go home. He did get him drunk, but still, Uriah would not go home. He slept at the gate.

Finally, the next morning, David wrote a letter to Joab, which he gave to Uriah to deliver. It was literally Uriah's death decree. In it, David told Joab to put Uriah on the front lines of the fiercest battle, and then withdraw from him so he could be killed. This is exactly what happened. Uriah was killed in battle.

Now, David was not only guilty of adultery, but also of the premeditated murder of Uriah. II Samuel 11:27 says, "But the Lord was very displeased with what David had done." David's response to hearing of Uriah's death was very flippant and insensitive. While he had grieved deeply for Saul and Abner (his rivals in II Samuel 1), he showed no grief for Uriah, a good man with strong spiritual character. David had become callous to his own sin. Deliberate, repeated sinning had dulled David's sensitivity to God's law and other's rights. Many times the more you try to cover up a sin, the more insensitive you become toward it. Don't become hardened to sin! The longer you wait, the harder it becomes to get things right! Confess your sin to the Lord right away and get back in fellowship with Him. King David had abused his position of authority to get what he wanted. In a time when he should have taken heed, he fell.

God then sent the prophet Nathan to confront David with his sin. Nathan told a story of two men in a city, one very rich and the other very poor. One owned many flocks; the other had nothing but a little lamb. It was his children's pet and it was cuddled in their arms like a little baby. A guest arrived at the rich man's house, and instead of killing one of his own flock to feed him, he took the lamb from the poor man. David was furious and immediately proclaimed that man must be put to death and must repay four lambs to the poor man. Nathan, referring to what David did with Bathsheba and to Uriah, then shocks David and says, "You are the rich man!" He then begins to remind him how God has blessed him, made him king, delivered him from Saul, delivered him in war, etc. Then, by the word of the Lord, David is denounced for his sin, and that future rebellion would always be in David's house.

In II Samuel 12:13, David immediately says, "I have sinned against the Lord." Nathan then tells him he will not die for his sin, but the baby will. During this incident, David wrote Psalm 51, which gives valuable insight into his character and offers hope for us as well. He is so repentant, so sorrowful for his sin. More than that, he expresses deep concern that the Lord will leave him, showing how much he depended and needed God. We know that God forgives (I John 1:9) when we confess. We also know even though judgment came on David's house and that the baby died, and that insult was made to the name of the Lord, David was forgiven. David wrote Psalm 32 after he was forgiven, expressing his joy. Let us be on guard to never have to face a circumstance of our own making like David did. The good news is, if we do sin, not when but if, we can go to God the Father through Jesus and find forgiveness (I John 2:2).

Sin—Deal With It!

RE: II Samuel 13

As prophesied by the prophet Nathan, David's family problems were about to begin. David was about to face sins in his own family very similar to those he had committed earlier as we read in II Samuel 13.

It seems as if the sin in his life became magnified in the lives of his children. As a parent, it is important to always live by God's standards, giving a good example to our children to follow, even if we have sinned ourselves. In this chapter, Amnon, David's son, was literally obsessed with his half-sister, Tamar. Along with his cousin, Jonadab, they plotted a way to trap her. Amnon played sick and had Tamar fix food for him in his room. When she brought the food to him, he approached her sexually, and when she refused, he raped her. Immediately, his "love" turned to hate. In reality his love was really lust. He became so angry that he threw Tamar out. She left crying, with her long robe with long sleeves (the custom of virgins in those days) now torn and with ashes on her head. The crimes Amnon committed were rape and incest, both strictly forbidden by God (Deuteronomy 25–29; 20:17). His rejection of Tamar was even a greater crime, because by throwing her out, he made it look as if she had made the shameful proposition to him. There were no witnesses on her behalf because he had gotten rid of all the servants. His crime ruined her life because she was no longer a virgin and no longer able to be given in marriage (Deuteronomy 22:23–28).

When Absalom found out that his sister had been raped, a seed of hatred was sown in him (II Samuel 13:22), which would eventually cause him to murder Amnon and turn against his father, the king. Although David was angry with Amnon, he did not punish him. According to God's law, David should have had Amnon banished (Leviticus 20:17). David could have hesitated because:

1. As his eldest son, he was next in line for the throne (I Chronicles 3:1).
2. He was guilty of a similar sin himself in his adultery with Bathsheba.

While David was unsurpassed as a king and military leader, he lacked the sensitivity and good judgment necessary for a godly husband and father. When we do not deal with sin, it will run rampant in our lives, and we will reap the corruption we have sown. This happened with David's family, as we shall see. Proverbs 28:13 says, "He that covereth his sins shall not prosper; but whoso confesseth and forsaketh them shall have mercy."

Hatred, a Seed
of Disaster

RE: II Samuel 13—15

I John 3:15 tells us, "Whosoever hateth his brother is a murderer." These words are literally an echo of Jesus' words in Matthew 5:21, 22. II Samuel 13:22 says, "Absalom hated Amnon because of what he had done to his sister Tamar" (that is, he raped her, stealing her virginity). Bitterness is as an evil cancer within you, and will eventually destroy you if not dealt with. Hebrews 12:15 teaches us not to let a "root of bitterness grow in us." This is precisely what happened to Absalom. While he had good reason to be angry, he did not have reason to hate Amnon. Instead of confronting him with his sin, he allowed his anger to turn to "deep hatred" (Living Bible). II Samuel 13:21 (Living Bible) says, "Absalom said nothing one way or the other about this to Amnon." This produced revenge and not resolution. In his heart, anger had turned to hatred, and a seed of disaster was sown. Absalom's plan was to kill him no matter how long he had to wait. And wait he did! Two years later he invited David, his father, to come to a celebration feast of the shearing of his sheep at Ephraim. King David refused to go, but thanked him for his kindness. Absalom then asked him to send Amnon in his stead. This was quite a surprise to David, but when Absalom kept pushing the issue, David gave in and sent Amnon and the rest of his sons.

Absalom had already told his servants that when Anmon got drunk, they were to kill him. This is exactly what they did. The rest of the family fled back to Jerusalem to report what had been done. Before they could arrive, someone had spread the rumor that all of David's sons had been killed. David jumped up, ripped off his robe, and fell prostrate to the ground, while all his servants and aides did the same.

Jonadab, David's nephew, arrived and said, "No, not all have been killed. It was Amnon who was killed. Absalom has been plotting this ever since Amnon raped Tamar" (II Samuel 13:32, 33). Imagine what Jonadab had done! He was the one who helped Amnon accomplish what he did to Tamar, and now he knew that Absalom was plotting to kill him.

Remember what John said. Hatred is just like murder. That terrible, revengeful spirit had gotten into Absalom and literally had turned him into a murderer before he ever committed the act. James 1:15 says, "Then when lust hath conceived [in this case the lust was anger, what it conceived was hatred] it bringeth forth sin [premeditated murder] and sin when it is finished bringeth forth death [the actual murdering]." These seeds many times take a while to grow, but they will grow if they are not dealt with. This was certainly the case with Absalom.

As Jonadab is telling David that only Amnon is dead and all the other brothers are fine; the brothers, close to the city, are on their way home, weeping. Absalom escaped to Geshur where he would stay with King Talmar for three years.

After all this time, General Joab realized how much David missed Absalom and sent a woman of Tehoa, with a reputation of being a woman of wisdom, to the king, in an attempt to convince him to send for Absalom. She told him a masterful story, and as she proceeded, he realized the story, similar to the one Nathan had told years before, was in direct reference to him. (Read II Samuel 14 for detailed information.) David called Joab and instructed him to bring Absalom back. Absalom returned, but David had instructed Joab that he was not to be seen at the palace. As David had not punished Anmon for his sin, when finally he allowed Absalom back, he did not speak to him for two years. When sin is ignored it will result in greater pain than if it is dealt with immediately.

Finally, after two years, Absalom grew tired of living in Jerusalem and not being able to talk to King David, his father. Scripture records in II Samuel 14:25 (Living Bible) that Absalom was a handsome specimen of manhood, and no one else received such praise. He cut his hair only once a year and only then because it weighed three pounds and was too heavy to carry around. This pride and vanity was going to do him in. He strongly and repeatedly urged Joab to get him an appointment (actually, he wanted a "trial" to see if he would be found guilty of murder) with David. When Joab persistently refused, Absalom set fire to his only barley field to get his attention. Now he had his opportunity to see David, but things would get much worse before getting better.

The Conspiracy of
a Rebel

RE: II Samuel 15

After two years of silence from his father David, Absalom, living in Jerusalem, finally got an appointment with his father. As we saw in our previous meditation, he accomplished this by setting Joab's field of barley on fire. II Samuel 14:33 says that when Absalom came in, he bowed down to David, and David kissed Absalom, signifying his forgiveness and reconciliation with the royal family. David sidestepped justice and repentance, thereby contributing to what Absalom was about to do. This is somewhat like the story of the prodigal son, with one exception. The prodigal son was repentant and did not seek anything for himself (Luke 15:21). Whatever he was given was by the love of his father. Absalom showed no remorse and no repentance for the murder he committed.

Sometime later on we see Absalom as the "proud" owner of a chariot (perhaps the first Israelite leader to acquire one). He has approximately fifty men around him as bodyguards. They cleared the way for him as he walked, and often would announce his name as he walked along. The chariot and fifty men provided a display of royal pomp that appealed to the people.

II Samuel 15:2 explains that Absalom would get up early in the morning and stand by the side of the road leading to the city gate. Whenever anyone came to bring a complaint (case) to the king, Absalom called him and expressed interest in his problem. The city gate was comparable to city hall and a shopping center combined. As the people would come with their cases, Absalom would side with them in an attempt to ingratiate himself with the people. He endorsed their grievances without any investigation into their legitimacy. Absalom presented himself as the solution to the people's problems. He was undermining the authority of the king and gaining the support of the crowd. II Samuel 15:5 describes how he would kiss the hand of a person as an outward symbol of humility. We already know of his pride and ego from previous chapters. Now notice what the Scripture says in II Samuel 15:6, that as Absalom showed this outward concern, he "stole the hearts of all the people of Israel." His handsome figure, his grand entrances, his public position of justice, and his seemingly warm and friendly embraces, were only part of a facade to steal the hearts of the people. The anger, resentment, and hate that drove him to kill his own brother in a wicked plot, now had driven him to rebellion and a hunger for power. His outward style and charm was a mask for his inward hypocrisy. His concern was not for people, but for power.

After four years, Absalom's plot had been carefully woven. Feeling confident, he asked the king if he could return to Hebron, his hometown, to repay a vow. We do not know if, in fact, there was a vow. What he really wanted to accomplish was to gain more favor in his hometown to fulfill his plan to overthrow the king. When David agreed to let him go, he sent spies to every part of Israel to incite rebellion against the king. In II Samuel 15:10, Absalom said, "As soon as you hear the trumpets you will know Absalom is crowned king in Hebron." Two hundred men from Jerusalem had accompanied him to Hebron, but they were unaware of his intentions. While he was offering the sacrifice, he sent for Ahithophel, one of David's counselors. Ahithophel declared his allegiance to Absalom, as did more and more others.

The conspiracy was now very strong. David, hearing of this rebellion, decided to flee from Jerusalem immediately in an attempt to preserve the city and his men from destruction. How sad to see the king once again on the run, this time from his own son. We see him in the wilderness with many people who have followed, with rent clothes and in mourning. It was at this time that he wrote many Psalms (39, 41, 55, 61, 62, 63). Even though David had made mistakes with his family, Absalom was in sin. Rebellion is as the sin of witchcraft, as we found out with Saul. People who are committed to God become better in problems; those who are not become bitter. David's steadfast character is about to be displayed once again. As in every other horrible case prior, his trust in God would get him through. Is your trust in God doing the same for you?

Do Not Follow Foolish Advice

RE: II Samuel 15, 16

After Absalom had impressed many of the people with his good looks and charisma, he asked to go to Hebron and was granted permission by David. There, he begins to set up his self-proclaimed rule. The anointing was on David, and though sin and indecisiveness had many times clouded his life, he still had a heart after God. Knowing now that Absalom, his rebellious and proud son, was about to come down to Jerusalem for an attack, David and his men fled. Along with his loyal followers, he now found himself as before with Saul, on the run, weeping as he went, mourning with his feet bare and head covered.

The Bible calls David, "A man after God's own heart" in Acts 13:22. That didn't mean his life was free of troubles. His life was full of highs and lows. Some of David's troubles were the result of his own sins, and some were the result of the sins of others. The lesson of David's life, although it seems out of control at times, is his persistent faith and confidence in God to bring him through. Psalms 55:16 (a Psalm written when David was fleeing from Absalom) says, "But I will call upon the Lord to save me—and he will" (Living Bible).

Even though David is weeping and mourning, he has the presence of mind to pray. His prayer is quite significant and quite interesting. Someone told David that Ahithophel (David's former advisor and the grandfather of Bathsheba) was backing Absalom. Apparently, he had been secretly backing Absalom's rebellion in the planning stage, perhaps for retaliation for what David had done to Bathsheba and Uriah. It seems that this betrayal by Ahithophel of David, as a close friend and trusted advisor, prompted David to write about him as a "close friend" in Psalm 41:9; 55:12–14 (also referred to as Messianic references to Jesus and Judas).

Notice David's prayer in II Samuel 15:31; "O Lord, turn Ahithophel's counsel into foolishness" (New Intrnational Version). Before David could reach the top of the Mount of Olives, he had an answer. Hushai, David's most trusted advisor (See I Chronicles 27:33, where he is called, "The King's Friend"), was waiting for him at the top of the Mount of Olives. David's prayer would be carried out through him. God always answers prayer, even though at times circumstances must be dealt with first. In this case, the answer was immediate. James 5:16 in the Amplified Bible states, "The earnest (heartfelt, continued) prayer of a righteous man makes tremendous power available—dynamic in its working." David sends Hushai to Jerusalem to tell Absalom, "I will counsel you as I did your father. Then you can frustrate and counter Ahithophel's advice" (II Samuel 15:33, 34). He then said to tell Zadok and Abiathar, the priests, of Absalom's plans to capture him, because they would send their sons to find David and tell him what was going on!

Hushai goes into the city of Jerusalem, presents himself before the king, and proclaims, "Long live the king." Absalom asks why he is not with the king. Hushai responds, "I helped your father, and now I'll help you."

Absalom seems to accept this answer. Then he turns to Ahithophel, and asks him, "What shall I do next?" Ahithophel comes up with advice to take twelve thousand men and immediately attack David and his men while they are weary and discouraged. This was to throw them into a panic. Ahithophel then says he will kill the king, save every one else, and restore them to Absalom. The Bible says Absalom and all the elders approved the plan, but Absalom said, "Ask Hushai the Archite what he thinks about this." God had arranged this situation so that Absalom was asking the person who had come to disrupt his plans. No matter how dark the situation is, trust God; He is in control. "The heart of the king is in the hand of the Lord."

Hushai's advice appealed to Absalom's pride. With flattery, he suggests not to send his men alone, but for Absalom to go himself, saying, "Surely your father is a mighty warrior and no one is a match to him." He suggests great glory for Absalom. Instead of listening to Ahithophel's advice, he submits to his own vanity, which is about to become his own trap. Proverbs 18:12 teaches us, "Pride ends in destruction." This is certainly an appropriate epitaph for Absalom. The Bible says, "Then Absalom and all the men of Israel said, "Hushai's advice is better than Ahithophel's." For the Lord had arranged to defeat the counsel of Ahithophel, which really was the better plan, so that he could bring disaster on Absalom (II Samuel 17:14, 15) Faith and confidence in God sets His plan in motion for us. The Lord was going to frustrate the proud and egotistical heart of Absalom. Thank God He has everything under control!

Be Sure Your Sin Will Find You Out

RE: II Samuel 17, 18

Since Absalom committed to follow Hushai's advice, which was arranged by God to trap Absalom, his fall was just a matter of time. The Bible says, "Fools make a mock at sin." In other words, they think they can do anything and get away with it. Absalom had been on a rebellious rampage, dividing the kingdom and allegiance to his own father. David truly loved his son, yet here was Absalom turning the hearts of the people against him. Sometimes it looks as if God is allowing people to get away with things, or it seems as if nothing is happening (Note the complaint of the prophet Habakkuk in Habakkuk chapter 1). Absalom was going to set his own trap. David still had loyal followers and Hushai was one of them. Having arranged for word of Absalom's plans to be carried back to David, he and his troops would be ready to ambush Absalom and his army.

The Bible says in II Samuel 18:6–9, "So the battle began in the forest of Ephraim, and the Israeli troops were beaten back by David's men. There was a great slaughter and twenty thousand men laid down their lives that day. The battle raged all across the countryside, and more men disappeared in the forest than were killed. During the battle Absalom came upon some of David's men and he fled on his mule, it went beneath the thick boughs of a great Oak tree, and his hair caught in the branches."

Joab, although asked by David to spare his life, plunges three daggers into him and kills him. Absalom's impressive head of hair, once the pride of his life, was responsible for his death. How ironic that the very sin of pride that caused him to rebel and divide the kingdom became responsible for his death. His sin found him out. The Bible records many rebellions, the majority of them being against God's chosen leaders. Although they were sometimes successful, the rebel's life usually came to a violent end.

Examine the Scripture that says, "He that being often reproved hardeneth his neck, shall suddenly be cut off, and that without remedy." We cannot take lightly the things of God. Proverbs 6:18 explains that one of the things God hates is "a heart that deviseth wicked imaginations."

Mighty Men

RE: II Samuel 19—24

The next several chapters of II Samuel are really an appendix to the book. The events that are described are not presented in chronological order. They tell of David's exploits at various times during his reign. There are some very interesting things that happen, which have great spiritual and some prophetic application. It is notable that in David's return to Jerusalem, after defeating Absalom, Sheba had incited another rebellion against him. David had sent Joab, Abishai, and a small army after him. Joab and his troops besieged Abel, where Sheba was hiding, until the people of Abel ordered him killed, not wanting to see any bloodshed in their city.

It is important to remember that when we win a battle, it does not mean there will not be more. We must keep in our hearts at all times what I Peter 5:8, 9 declares; "Be sober, be vigilant; because your adversary the devil, as a roaring lion, walketh about, seeking whom he may devour: Whom resist steadfast in the faith, knowing that the same afflictions are accomplished in your brethren that are in the world." Another good thing to keep in mind is Luke 4, where Jesus defeated Satan in the wilderness. Verse 13 says, "He left him for a season." David continually faced conflict and chaos. Some of the conflict came as a result of his own sin. There was other conflict that arose simply because Satan wanted this man after God's heart defeated, since he was in the lineage of Christ.

One of the more interesting themes seen throughout David's life is the loyalty of those who served around him. While there were some who betrayed him, it would benefit us to see the impact of these mighty men. "Mighty men" may seem like a strange description, as we will see that most of them surely did not begin as mighty men.

During the time David was being hunted by Saul, he gradually built a fighting force of several hundred men. Some were relatives, others were outcasts from society, and many were in trouble with the law. They all shared at least one thing in common—devotion and loyalty to David. Thank God we are what we are by the grace of God! We do not accomplish things because of "who" we are, but because of "whose" we are. These men developed elite military groups like "The Three" and "The Thirty" and were true heroes. The key verses are found in I Samuel 22:1, 2, describing how they got to David's side (Living Bible); "So David left Gath and escaped to the cave of Adullam, where his brothers and other relatives soon joined him." As they and others began coming, David became the leader of about four hundred men. What a way to start an army! We can say this was certainly a unique debut!

Scriptures give the impression that these men were motivated to greatness by the personal qualities of their leader. David inspired them to achieve beyond their goals and meet their true potential. David's effectiveness as a leader was certainly connected to his awareness of God's leading. As long as David was following his leader, he himself was a good leader. Greatness is often inspired by the quality and character of leadership. Although this group was rather small, their loyalty and courage truly made them able men. God is not looking as much for ability as He is for availability.

The great lesson for us to learn is that when we submit to God and His plan for our lives, "Little will become much when God is in it." It was a shepherd's staff in Moses' hand, an ox-goad in Shamgar's hand, the jawbone of an ass in Samson's hand, and a sling in David's hand. When we begin to realize that our confidence and trust in God is really more important than our degrees, our education, and our accomplishments, we will begin to see Bible results in our lives. May we never settle for mediocrity and be content to barely survive, for God has given us His formula for our success.

Although David's men were often outnumbered, and conditions and situations were contrary, they always came out on top. The outstanding lesson of David's mighty men is: If God could do those things in the Old Testament, and we are living under a better covenant in the New Testament (Hebrews 8:6), this certainly means that our success has already been made sure. May God give us willing hearts that will not be afraid to fulfill God's plan for our lives.

Remember that "willing" men will become "able" men when they put their trust and confidence in the Lord their God.

The Last Days of
a Champion

RE: II Samuel 24

The book of II Samuel describes David's reign. We have seen as we have studied highlights from this book that David was truly a man after God's heart (Acts 13:22). Since the Israelites first entered the Promised Land under Joshua they had been struggling to unite the land (nation) and drive out the wicked inhabitants. Now after more than four hundred years, Israel was finally at peace. David had accomplished what no leader before him, judge or king, had done. His administration was run on the principle of dedication to God, as well as the good (well-being) of the people. He was responsible for bringing the ark of God back to Israel. The many Psalms that David wrote are truly an indication of the heart he had towards God, and they display the relationship he had with God.

Yet we must point out that David often sinned. We know of his sin with Bathsheba and the planned death of Uriah, but even in the later days of his life we see error. He disobeyed God and took a census of the people. His motive was to glory in the size of his nation and army, its power and defenses. In doing this, he put faith in the size of his army rather than in God's ability to protect him, regardless of their number. Both David and Israel were guilty of sin (II Samuel 24:1). David's sin was pride. God gave David three choices of punishment for his sin. David chose the punishment that came directly from God. The other two punishments would come by the hands of men. Here is the secret of David's life; even in the midst of disobedience, he turned back to God, submitting himself into God's hands. If we do sin, we must remember never to run from Him, but run to Him.

Despite all the times he missed God, by admitting and confessing his sin, David always kept his heart open to God. As a young man, he had committed himself to God, and through thick and thin, was still committed to God, even as an old man. Let us always remember that, like David, we must keep the Lord always in our hearts. Matthew 6:33 says, "Seek ye first the kingdom of God and His righteousness, and all these things shall be added unto you."

FINAL
MEDITATIONS

Although cycles of sin, servitude and repentance plagued the Old Testament believer throughout the book of Judges, when repentance came, so did the blessing of God. From the Israelites up to King David, and all the way through the lineage of Jesus Christ, one truth holds constant; those who put their hope and trust in God, will NEVER be ashamed. Even when we fail, if our hearts are upright before God and we keep confidence in Him, He picks us up and makes our path straight again.

While I know you have been blessed by having taken the time to meditate on these life lessons from Old Testament history, my hope is that you grasp the reality of who God really is in your life. In these pages, we have celebrated victories of Old Testament champions and learned from fatal mistakes of fallen heroes, but the most common theme is to put all of our hope and confidence in the Lord God, Jehovah.

I have spent my life studying the Word of God and its history. It took many years to compile a book that would give you history and lineage of the Old Testament and make it easy to read and understand and very relevant to modern day life. The simple fact is—God's plan for man to succeed in every area of life has never changed and neither has the human heart. When we seek to know Him and His power—He never lets us down.

My prayer is that you will know Him, as never before, be strong and do exploits! As I have quoted from Jeremiah many times before, God's plan for His people has always been for good and not for evil; to give you hope and a future. You cannot lose when you take Him at His Word. I challenge you to review this book as often as you can to recount and remember our conquering, overcoming God who is now your personal God—for every day and every circumstance.

Notes

Prayer

Father, I thank You that You have given me Your Word to hide in my heart that I might not sin against You. I thank You that I have studied and shown myself approved unto You, that I might not be ashamed, and may rightly divide the Word of truth.

I thank you that like...

Samuel, I hear the voice of the Good Shepherd.

Solomon, I am wise, and I will teach my children Your ways.

David, I have a heart after God, and I am strong in the Lord.

Jonathan, I will be faithful to Your leaders.

Ruth, I have a heart to follow and I am loyal.

Gideon, I can do nothing without You, but with You I am a mighty man of valor, and I can do all things!

I will continue to grow in the grace and knowledge of the Lord Jesus Christ and be an example of a believer to the world!

In the name of Jesus, Amen.

For more information or for a FREE catalog:

Write To:
David T. Demola Ministries, Inc.
2707 Main Street
Sayreville, NJ 08872

Or Call:
732-727-9500